THE VOID

THE VOID

*Inner Spaciousness
and Ego Structure*

A. H. Almaas

SHAMBHALA
Boston & London
2003

Shambhala Publications
Horticultural Hall
300 Massachusetts Avenue
Boston, Ma. 02115
www.shambhala.com

Published by arrangement with Diamond Books

Cover design: Layna Berman

For permission to reprint excerpts, the author is grateful to the following:

Basic Books, Inc., Publishers for *The Psychological Birth of the Human Infant*, Mahler, Margaret S., et al., 1975; Doubleday & Company, Inc. for *Irrational Man*, Barrett, W., 1962; Gardner Press, Inc. for *Separation-Individuation*, Edward, Joyce, et al., 1981; International University Press, Inc. for *Psychoanalytic Explorations of Technique*, Blum, Harold P., 1980, for *Schizoid Phenomena, Object-Relations, and the Self*, Guntrip, Harry, 1969, for *The Restoration of the Self* and *The Analysis of the Self*, Kohut, Heinz, 1981, for *The Self and the Object World*, Jacobson, Edith, 1980; Jason Aronson for *Borderline Conditions and Pathological Narcissism*, Kernberg, Otto, 1975; W. W. Norton & Company, Inc. for *The Ego and the Id*, Freud, Sigmund, 1962; and The Psychoanalytic Quarterly Press and W. W. Norton & Company, Inc. for *The Problem of Anxiety*, Freud, Sigmund, 1963.

9 8 7 6 5 4 3 2 1

First Shambhala Edition
Printed in the United States of America

⊗ This edition is printed on acid-free paper that meets the
American National Standards Institute Z39.48 Standard.
Distributed in the United States by Random House, Inc.,
and in Canada by Random House of Canada Ltd

Library of Congress Cataloging-in-Publication Data
Almaas, A.H.
The void: inner spaciousness and ego structure/A.H. Almass.
p. cm.
Originally published: Berkeley, CA: Diamond Books: Almaas Publications, 1986.
Includes bibliographical references.
ISBN 0-936713-06-2 (pbk.)
1. Mind and body. 2. Space and time—Psychological aspects
3. Self-perception 4. Spiritual life 5. East and West I. Title.
BF161 A5 2000
150—dc21
00–040031

Dedicated to the following people who made it possible to transform the original manuscript into this book:

Marie Ali
Farouq Aqeel
Kristina Bear
Byron Brown
Alia Johnson
Duncan Scribner
Abdullah Zaman

TABLE OF CONTENTS

INTRODUCTION

to the

Diamond Mind Series

The Void is the first volume of the Diamond Mind Series. This series is a systematic presentation of a particular body of knowledge, which we call Diamond Mind, and its corresponding modus operandi, a way of working with people toward inner realization, which we call the Diamond Approach. The presentation is somewhat technical, and hence will be useful to psychologists, psychotherapists, educators and spiritual teachers, but is also accessible to the educated reader. This work is a response to an important need that is being felt in many quarters, a need for a spiritually informed psychology, or conversely, for a psychologically grounded spirituality. This perspective does not separate psychological and spiritual experience, and hence sees no dichotomy between depth psychology and spiritual work. Through a creative critique and investigation, this system takes some of the elements of depth psychology, particularly those of ego psychology and object relations theory, and extends them into realms of the human psyche which are usually considered the domain of religion, spirituality and metaphysics.

This body of knowledge is not an integration or synthesis of modern depth psychology and traditional spiritual understanding. The inclination to think in terms of integration of the two is due to the prevailing belief in the dichotomy between the fields of psychology and spirituality, a dichotomy in which the Diamond Mind understanding does not participate.

The Diamond Mind knowledge is a multifaceted understanding of the nature of man, his consciousness or psyche, and the potential for expansion of his capacity for experience and inner development. These several points regarding the nature of this understanding will help to place it in context:

1. This knowledge includes an understanding of normal psychological functioning which also sheds light on some prevalent mental disorders. It adopts many of the findings of modern depth psychology, situating them in a more comprehensive view of man and also establishing their relevance for the pursuit of deeper truths about human nature beyond the levels psychology generally penetrates.

2. The psychological understanding is set within a metapsychological perspective that includes a broad outline of the domains of experience and functioning of the human psyche or soul. This metapsychology is not spelled out in any one of the volumes of the series, but is gradually developed throughout its several books.

3. This metapsychology is in turn set within a metaphysical outlook in which psychological experience is situated within a phenomenology of Being.

4. This work demonstrates that what is usually considered psychological investigation can arrive at dimensions of experience which have always been considered to be the product of spiritual practice or discipline. The psychological work is seen here not as an adjunct to spiritual practice, but as a spiritual practice on its own. This is the specific contribution of the Diamond Mind body of knowledge which prompted the idea of this series.

5. Not only *can* psychological investigation lead to realms of experience previously relegated to the spiritual, this work shows that when psychological understanding is refined by an openness to one's spiritual nature, such investigation, if pursued

deeply, *inevitably will* penetrate into the realm of spiritual, religious or mystical understanding. In the course of such exploration one result is that many currently prevalent psychological dysfunctions, such as some forms of narcissism and schizoid isolation, are revealed as direct consequences of spiritual alienation, which thus cannot be truly resolved by traditional psychotherapy.

6. This body of work includes a systematic understanding of the domain of spiritual experience, the realm of Being, that can be described in detail in modern psychological language. Thus it shows that this domain of experience need not be vague, symbolic or incommunicable. It also includes an exploration of the relationships between this domain of experience and the usual psychological dimension of experience, shedding light on the nature of ego structure and identity. Thus the dimension of Being can be included in some modes of psychological research and investigation.

7. The presentation in the various volumes of the series attempts to illustrate methods of investigation, as well as the clinical and scientific bases for our conclusions, within a conceptually logical treatment of the various subject matters. However, because of the nature of the field of inquiry, the reader may well be aware of an experiential impact that cannot always be separated from the conceptual knowledge. This points to a particular quality of the Diamond knowledge: it is an experiential knowledge that is immediate and intimately human, but which can be elaborated conceptually.

It is my wish that this knowledge will be useful in refining and deepening our understanding of who and what we are as human beings. Perhaps it will make it possible for more of us to actualize our rich potential and to live more complete lives.

A.H. Almaas
Berkeley, California
November 1987

INTRODUCTION

One of the great tasks of modern Western psychology is to integrate into itself the depths of human understanding and freedom of spirit discovered by the major world religious traditions, to make psychology not just a cure for mundane human distress but to bring forth from it liberation and wholeness of the human spirit. It is toward this end that A.H. Almaas has directed his life work and *The Void* represents the result of one aspect of that study from which we can learn a great deal.

In this book, as in his other works (*The Elixir of Enlightenment, Essence*), Almaas brings together two qualities which are rarely combined in modern research, a profound theoretical understanding of mind and mental development coupled with a rich background in working privately and in groups with students. Using concepts and experiences drawn from contemporary object relations theory and Freudian-based ego psychology, case studies from his practice, and teachings from the highest levels of Buddhist and other Eastern practices, he challenges us to look not only at the personality and content of mind but at the underlying nature of Mind itself.

In a remarkable and direct way, Almaas introduces us to the space or ground of Mind within which mental structures operate. He shows how inner spaciousness can be experienced in somatic, psychological and spiritual ways, details some of the many levels of inner space and, more importantly, illustrates how these experiences of space can lead to fundamental healing and integration of our being. This experiential understanding of non-identification with content, discovering the pattern of object relations and self-representations as grasped images in the mind, is called the Truth of Selflessness, the central key to the Buddha's realization and enlightenment. From the experience of the Mind ground (the inherent emptiness of mind and its objects), there spontaneously arises a liberating sense of wholeness and true well-being, as well as strength, compassion and other natural qualities which Almaas calls our Essential State(s).

While this book is an important contribution to the psychological understanding of mind, it is also a plea for dissolving the false split between psychology and spiritual life. In a world where we have not dealt with our shadows, where the split of body and mind, light and dark, persona and shadow have led to the threatening devastation of the nuclear arms race, our way to recovering wholeness and sanity is only by means of healing these splits.

The deep spiritual and psychological knowledge which Almaas brings to this work places him in the forefront of a new movement in psychology which draws on the practices and understanding of ancient and Eastern traditions and the best of contemporary and Western psychology as well. For the serious student of psychology there is much to learn from this work, and no doubt more good things to come from Almaas in the future.

Jack Kornfield, Ph.D.
Dharma Foundation
San Anselmo, California
1985

PART ONE

The Void and the Self

CHAPTER ONE

The Mind

In ordinary usage, the word "mind" refers to thoughts, the thinking process, or the thinking apparatus. But there are other usages: in the East, for example, "mind" includes more than just the thinking sphere. And here in the West as well, the word often has a larger meaning. In fact, most of the depth psychologies, and the social sciences in general, use the term "mind" to include all inner experience. The mind is then taken to be the field or sphere of our thoughts, images, feelings, emotions, sensations, and perceptions, plus the apparatus or agent that deals with all these impressions. This "mind" is connected not only to the brain, but to the totality of the nervous system.

Here, we will use the term "mind" in this larger, more inclusive sense. We will also be open to modifications or extensions of this definition.

Although in the East the term refers to an even larger sphere of experience than we describe above, the main difference between the Western and Eastern idea of "mind" is more a matter of emphasis. The Western casual use of "mind" generally refers to the content of experience, while the Eastern use of the word usually emphasizes the substratum, or the container, of experience. The Western "mind" is the stuff of experience itself, the inner events, the thoughts, feelings, sensations and perceptions; in the East, "mind" is seen more as the ground of all experience. These two emphases exemplify the traditional divergence between Eastern and Western character, ideals, values, philosophies, psychologies, religions, and so on. Today, however, this divergence is no longer maintained by geography; it is becoming more obvious that this difference is a matter of emphasis and point of view. The Western mind is increasingly prevalent in the East, and the Eastern one in the West.

Our interest here is to show the relationship between these two points of view, and to demonstrate how to move from one to the other. Understanding this relationship will eliminate the artificial divergence between the two perspectives, and will free our minds in terms of how we are able to think about human experience.

Our objective in this book, however, is much more ambitious than achieving this understanding and integration of the two points of view regarding the mind. We are interested in seeing how this understanding will make it possible for us to eliminate the usually accepted contradistinctions between mind and spirit, between psychology and religion, and between psychological understanding and spiritual (essential) development.

We are not going to perform a "synthesis" between psychological understanding and spiritual development. Nor are we going to claim that psychological understanding is identical to spiritual development (because it is not). We will show, rather, in a precise and verifiable way, that the distinction between the psychological and the spiritual paths to understanding and development is only the result of an artificial separation. What is usually seen as two processes is actually one.

In the past few decades, there have been many attempts to integrate and synthesize the Eastern and Western points of view regarding mind. Our understanding is that these attempts, although at times useful, are bound to be partial and incomplete, because they generally assume that the spheres of psychology and spirituality are actually two.

CHAPTER TWO

Depth Psychology
and the Mind

Depth psychology in the West has primarily concerned itself with the mind as content of experience. This point of view is valuable, but must be placed in its correct perspective. Psychoanalysis in particular, starting with the monumental discoveries and formulations of Sigmund Freud, has contributed the primary and most useful understanding of the human mind in this century. Freud's contributions not only expanded our understanding of the human mind, but also became fertile ground for numerous psychotherapeutic approaches which have helped to alleviate the suffering of many people.

Freud and his immediate disciples (some of whom later developed their own systems) studied the mind as content and made the first cogent formulation for understanding this psychic content. Freud was interested in understanding the mind in terms of its functions, forces, processes, conflicts, and the like. This interest stemmed not only from the wish to help his suffering patients, but also from his deep love of understanding and truth. He wanted to understand human nature; in that, he succeeded profoundly, leaving behind a legacy of understanding that had never existed before him, and paving the way for a whole new way of looking at human beings.

Freud formulated a wide-ranging theory which sought to explain the mind in terms of instinctual forces, inner conflicts, consciousness and unconsciousness, and so on. The final major formulation of his work appeared in *The Ego and the Id*. He saw the personality (or in his terms, the mind) as a structure—a psychic structure—composed of three units: id, ego, and superego. (Literally translated, the words he used for these three concepts are the It, the I, and the Over-I.)

> We shall now look upon an individual as a psychical id, unknown and unconscious, upon whose surface rests the ego, developed from its nucleus the perceptual Pcpt. system. If we make an effort to represent this pictorially, we may add that the ego does not completely envelop the id, but only does so to the extent to which the system Pcpt. forms its [the ego's] surface, more or less as the germinal disc rests upon the ovum. The ego is not sharply separated from the id; its lower portion merges into it. (Sigmund Freud, *The Ego and the Id*, p. 14.)

> If the ego were merely the part of the id modified by the influence of the perceptual system, the representative in the mind of the real external world, we should have a simple state of things to deal with. But there is a further complication.

> The considerations that led us to assume the existence of a grade in the ego, a differential within the ego, which may be called the "ego ideal" or "superego," have been stated elsewhere. (Ibid., p. 18.)

So for Freud, the psyche or the mind consists of a structure composed of three units: the id, which is the reservoir of all

5

instinctual forces and energies, and which is merged with the physical organism; the ego, which forms mostly the functional self that is in direct contact with the external world; and the superego, which is the moral and ethical element of the Ego. This understanding of the mind as a tripartite psychic structure became the most important and most useful formulation in depth psychology. It became the basis for psychoanalysis and the psychotherapies springing from it or borrowing from it.

Later psychologists such as Jung, Reich and Perls developed other systems, but in general their work was not in contradiction to Freud's basic formulations about the psychic structure, and the basic Western approach to mind was retained.

In sum, this monumental contribution of Freud's, although of great theoretical and practical value, did remain within the Western conception of mind. The psychic structure is simply the structure of the content of experience. It is the pattern or patterning of the content of mind and experience.

CHAPTER THREE

Ego Psychology
and the Mind

---

reud did not, however, study how this structure develops.
He studied the mind in terms of the psychic structure in order
to understand repression and neurosis, and to understand
the process of psychotherapy. He understood neurosis, and mental conflict in general, to be a result of the dynamic interaction
between the units of this psychic structure.

It fell to the ego psychologists to make a detailed study of this
structure and its development through childhood experience. Ego
psychology developed as a branch of depth psychology concerned with the development of mental structure, in particular with
the development of the ego and the sense of identity or self.

Many psychologists contributed to the understanding of this
developmental psychology: Heinz Hartmann, Rene Spitz, Edith
Jacobson, D.W. Winnicott, P. Greenacre, and many others. The

most comprehensive and widely used formulation of the process of ego development is that of Margaret S. Mahler, whose work describes in detail the separation-individuation process.

> Through systematic observational studies of children and their parents, utilizing free-floating psycho-analytic observation and a predetermined experimental design, Mahler has detailed a complex developmental sequence to which she has given the name separation-individuation. Her work affirms Freud's recognition of the significance of infantile experiences for later development.
>
> Separation-individuation involves progression along two tracks. Separation refers to the child's movement from fusion with the mother; individuation consists of those steps that lead to the development of an individual's own personal and unique characteristics. Moving from autism to symbiosis, through four subphases of separation-individuation, namely differentiation, practicing, rapprochement, and a fourth open-ended subphase, the child advances to a position of on-the-way to object constancy . . . which represents a beginning sense of the self as separate from others, continuous in time and space. This process, in turn, encompasses an increasing capacity to retain an ongoing sense of sameness, despite fluctuations in emotions and bodily feelings, or external surroundings. . . .
>
> Favorable negotiation of the separation-individuation sequence leads to psychological birth and helps to promote the structuralization of the mental apparatus, the development of adaptive capacity, the acquisition of identity, and the resources for mutuality in human relationships. (Joyce Edward, *Separation-Individuation*, pp. xiii-xiv.)

Thus, according to ego psychology, a stable sense of identity or separate self is not something that the human being is born with, but is a result of a developmental process—what Mahler has called separation-individuation. At birth there is no awareness of an entity that is separate from its environment. A psychologically separate identity develops slowly as the infant interacts with its environment, especially with its mother.

Thus the identity, with its mental apparatus (psychic structure), is a construction in the mind. The particular structure of the mind, the particular patterning of the content of the psyche (ultimately resulting in the sense of self), is something that develops, something that grows. It is then something not ready-made at physical birth. This is why Mahler speaks of "psychological birth."

Here we digress to point out a source of confusion about the term "ego." Readers who know both the spiritual and psychological literatures will find the term freely used in both, but with no general agreement on what the term refers to. This ambiguity often leads to confusion. The literature on spiritual development, on essential or inner development, on all matters of religious concern, generally uses the term "ego" to mean something which is seen as the barrier to spiritual realization. The literature on depth psychology, however, uses the term with a very different meaning. The ego referred to by Freud, and which ego psychology studies, is not the ego which is the barrier to spiritual development. They are two different concepts. The psychoanalytic term "ego" refers, rather, to the functional self, which is the site, organizer, and coordinator of the functions of perception, memory, mobility, and so on.

There is, however, a concept in depth psychology and ego psychology that coincides with the ego of spiritual literature: it is called the "ego-identity," and is sometimes referred to as the sense of self, or the sense of identity. This sense of self or separate identity is the main concern of ego developmental theory. This identity is, in fact, the acme, the most important outcome of ego development. It is ultimately the organizing center of the psychic apparatus. This psychic apparatus includes as one of its units the Freudian ego. In other words, the Freudian ego is part of the mind, is a structure or a structured process in it, while the self is a sense of identity and a center of action.

The exact sense in which the ego identity is a barrier to spiritual development will become clear in later chapters.

CHAPTER FOUR

Object Relations Theory

A further development of psychoanalytic developmental psychology (ego psychology) is object relations theory, represented, at the present time, by Margaret Mahler and Otto Kernberg, among others. Object relations theory takes Mahler's formulation of ego development and applies it to the specific understanding of how the psychic structure develops. The theory is that the psychic apparatus develops out of object relations, i.e., out of the relation of the infant to the external human object, the mother.

The formulations of object relations theory, as put forth by Kernberg, are extremely useful for our present exploration of the relationship of the psychic structure (and its sense of identity) to the notion of the mind as the ground of experience, because they provide specific, detailed descriptions of the development of the identity, and also form the basis for some of our experiential techniques for exploring the ego identity.

In the words of Otto Kernberg,

> Object relations theory considers the psychic appa-
> ratus as originating in the earliest stage of a process of
> internalization of object relations. This process covers,
> roughly speaking, the first three years of life and results
> in the formation of substructures of the psychic appa-
> ratus that will gradually differentiate. The stages of
> development of internalized object relations—that is, the
> stages of infantile autism, symbiosis, separation-indi-
> viduation, and object constancy—reflect the vicissitudes
> of the earliest substructures of the psychic apparatus.
> Discrete units of self-representation, object-representa-
> tion, and an affect disposition linking them are the basic
> object relations derived substructures that gradually
> evolve into more complex substructures (such as real-
> self and ideal-self, the real-object and ideal-object rep-
> resentations). Eventually, they will become integrated
> as intrapsychic structures in the ego, superego and id.
> (Harold Blum, Editor, *Psychoanalytic Explorations of
> Technique: Discourse on the Theory of Therapy*, pp.
> 207–208.)

To understand how the psychic structure (and thus the sense
of identity) develops, we need first to understand what an object
relation is. According to Kernberg, an object relation consists of
three parts: a self-representation, an object-representation, and an
affect (a certain emotional content) linking the two. A representation of self or object means an image, partial or total, of the self
or object. This image is not necessarily always visual or mental.
It can be emotional, tactile, or auditory. It is really an impression
of the self or object. Edith Jacobson describes the origins and
nature of the self-representation thus:

> The image of our self issues from two sources: first,
> from a direct awareness of our inner experiences, of sen-
> sations, of emotional and thought processes, of functional
> activity; and second, from indirect self perception and
> introspection, i.e., from the perception of our bodily and

> mental self as an object. Since for obvious reasons our capacity for detachment from our own self is at best very limited, our self-cognizant functions contribute only moderately to our conception of the self. Thus, the self-representation will never be strictly "conceptual." . . . The kernels of the early infantile self-images are the memory traces of pleasurable and unpleasurable sensations, which under the influence of autoerotic and of beginning functional activities and of playful general body investigation become associated with body images. (Edith Jacobson, *The Self and the Object World*, p. 20.)

Because any experience, whether pleasurable or not, leaves its memory trace as a certain impression of oneself, a certain impression of the other person or object, and an affect between the two, Kernberg's triad of the self-representation, the object-representation and the affect become the building blocks of the infant's psychic structure. So as the infant grows and receives impressions, many units of such triads form, these being units of object relations. In time, the various object representations fuse to make an overall object-image, and the various self-representations also fuse to make a total and cohesive self-image. This happens in the fourth and last stage of the separation-individuation process. In Margaret Mahler's words:

> From the point of view of the separation-individuation process, the main task of the fourth subphase is two-fold: 1) the achievement of a definite, in certain aspects lifelong, individuality, and 2) the attainment of a certain degree of object constancy. . . . As far as the self is concerned, there is a far-reaching structuralization of the ego, and there are definite signs of internalization of parental demands indicating the formation of superego precursors. . . . The last sub-phase (roughly the third year of life) is an extremely important intrapsychic developmental period, in the course of which a stable sense of entity (self-boundaries) is attained. (Margaret Mahler, et al., *The Psychological Birth of the Human Infant*, p. 109.)

What matters here for our discussion is that the sense of entity and identity (self-boundaries) is established gradually in the first three years of life, and that it is a process of fusion of many separate self-images into a total overall self-image. This self-image is not the external image that most people think of as "self-image"; it is more of an inner, comprehensive, mostly unconscious image of oneself, of which the external image (basically the social facade) is just a part.

Thus the entire world-view of a person, the structure of his world, so to speak, consists of this overall self-image plus the total constellation of object images, in relation to each other.

CHAPTER FIVE

Self-Images and Boundaries

After consolidation, the self-image not only gives the individual his sense of personal identity, but determines more than anything else his subsequent experience of himself, his life, and his environment. It determines his sense of being, his inner experience, and everything else about him. The self-image is constituted, as Mahler says, of self-boundaries: not only spatial boundaries, but all the boundaries that determine the range of the individual's experience, perception, and actions. For example, if an individual has a self-image of being weak, he will tend not to do things that he believes require strength. Likewise, a self-image of being stupid will inhibit a person from learning things that he believes require intelligence, so that he will actually not understand and will behave in a stupid way when confronted with such things.

Self-boundaries determine even what one is able to think. While it is true that different impressions stimulate different thoughts in the same person, still these thoughts are pretty much determined by the person's sense of who he is, that is, his self-image. So the thoughts that go through a person's mind are not really accidental, chaotic, or disconnected, although they may sometimes appear so. They appear chaotic because a large segment of the self-image is unconscious or preconscious, and thus shapes thoughts and experiences in a way that the conscious mind cannot be aware of. This fact makes it possible for a person, by careful observation of the patterns and trends in his thoughts, to gain much information concerning his sense of identity.

We usually think of a positive or negative self-image. Indeed, some boundaries can be seen as "good," as healthy or useful; others are more obviously limiting or false. But they remain boundaries, whether we call them good or bad. Some boundaries allow more freedom than others, but every individual has specific boundaries which limit his particular experience and action.

The limitations that such boundaries or self-images dictate can be seen easily in the emotional and psychological spheres. Let us take, for example, the case of a man who unconsciously believes he is small and weak. This belief is almost certain to be accompanied by a related body image—he will see himself as smaller than he really is, and underestimate his actual physical strength and capacity. This self-image will also probably include a sense of inadequacy about his sexuality and an experience of a child's penis or of an empty, dark hole where his penis is. This unconscious self-image dictates a conscious experience of being weak, passive, inadequate, lacking virility, and so on. Even if this self-image does not cause great suffering—although it usually does—it will definitely limit the experience and growth of such a man, more fundamentally than is usually assumed, in a way which only a man who fully accepts his penis can appreciate.

In object relations theory, self-image is usually looked at only from the perspective of how, when, and how well it is developed. We now ask a different kind of question: What do the boundaries of the self-image bound? We don't mean here how it bounds our experience or capacities; the question addresses a more fundamental level.

We know that self-image is a content of the mind that determines the nature of further contents of the mind, as we have seen. Our question here pertains more to the nature of the mind than to its content. Here we depart from the usual range of psychoanalytic theory, which generally doesn't question the nature of the mind at these levels.

In our investigation of the relation of self-image to the nature of the mind, and of how this self-image limits our perception of the mind, we will use both the theories and techniques of psychoanalytic object relations theory to gain insight into the nature of the mind and to point towards an actual lived experience of this nature. Conversely, this insight will deepen and refine the findings of object relations theory and ego psychology in general.

CHAPTER SIX

Self-Image and Space

W hereas object relations theory concerns itself with the development of the psychic apparatus or structure, our inquiry here is into the actual material of the psychic structure, into the ontological aspect of it. What is the mind, what is it made of, and how does self-image determine our perception of it? In other words, what is the mind besides its content? Where does this content exist?

One way of approaching the question is to investigate what happens when the self-image changes, i.e., when some of its boundaries are removed or modified. We already know how modification of the self-image can change a person's experience and action in the world. This is, in fact, one way of seeing the action of any kind of psychotherapy. As some of the boundaries imposed on the individual by his self-image are dissolved, he gains greater freedom of perception and action. For instance, as the "weak" person understands his "weakness," as he sees its genesis and understands its psychodynamics, this boundary of "weakness" is challenged and gradually dissolves. As the person stops thinking of himself as "weak," his actions in the world change. In fact, he starts acting in ways that he had never thought he could, taking actions that he had thought only "strong" people could take, or even doing things that he had never thought anyone could do. Anyone who has participated in any kind of therapy, or is himself a therapist, or has experienced or seen a change of self-image, knows this very well.

Since our interest here is the nature of the mind, we will concern ourselves more with a person's inner perception of himself than with external changes. A person whose "weak" self-image is dissolving sees and feels that he is "stronger," more capable, freer. His direct sense of himself, his inner experience, is of greater relaxation and decreased tension, both mental and physical. As a result, especially when this change of self-image is accepted, he feels his body and mind are more comfortable, bigger, roomier, more expanded. In the dissolution of a self-boundary there usually involves, sooner or later, a sense of expansion, of experiencing oneself as more spacious. Of course, it is likely that anxieties will arise in response to the expansion, anxieties which will be experienced as contraction, particularly in borderline personality structures, as we will discuss later. For now, we will consider only the relatively stable psychic structure.

We want to stress this experience of expansion, not just in the field of action in the world, but more significantly for our discussion, in the intimate experience of one's body and mind. The body feels roomier and the mind less cluttered and more open.

In our example, we see a direct relation between the removal of self-boundaries and the experience of greater freedom and spaciousness. This is a very consistent phenomenon in persons involved in psychotherapy or spiritual work. It is in fact safe to assert that the sense of spaciousness is directly proportional to the expansion of self-boundaries. Of course, as we have said, in rare instances this sense of spaciousness is not directly experienced, but we will understand as we go on that this does not contradict our basic description of the process.

As the boundaries of the self are pushed further and further out, a progressively greater sense of spaciousness results. In fact, the experience of spaciousness is nothing more than the direct inner experience of what is generally called self-expansion. This expansion may also result in an increase in the sense of one's depth, richness, or refinement, but we will leave these aspects of expansion until later, when we will show their relation to spaciousness.

Lest the reader take the "sense of spaciousness" to be abstract or metaphorical, we will give here a case history which makes clearer the nature of this experience.*

Sandra is a beautiful married woman of thirty. She has been working with me on self-understanding for a little over two years using various modalities and techniques. Here we find her struggling with and attempting to understand her feelings of inferiority, worthlessness, dependency, neediness, and emptiness. She is at the moment telling me about her suffering of the past few days as such feelings become more and more conscious. Her work on understanding has taught her to experience her state with a measure of disidentification. She breaks down crying at feeling empty. I ask her where in her body she feels the emptiness. She starts shaking, as if shivering, in different places in her body. She particularly feels her spine shaking. After a while she feels as if she has no spine; she is aware of emptiness at the lower back. She observes that she feels empty in the belly and pelvic region. I ask her to focus her attention more in that region.

She feels an emptiness in her lower belly. The emptiness becomes more specific; she actually physically feels a hole in her pelvis starting at the genitals. The entire area of her genitals feels like an emptiness, an empty hole. There is nothing there, according

---

* The case histories presented here are from written reports or transcripts of students' work with the author. The students work in group settings and in private sessions (which often involve breathing techniques) with the author and his colleagues. Students engage in a systematic practice of meditation and other traditional techniques, and pursue a deep psychodynamic exploration of the personality.

to her perception. This scares her and intensifies the shaking in her body. She now realizes, however, how her sense of herself as incomplete, as missing something, as inferior to others, and as empty, is based on a physical body-image of having an empty hole at the region of her genitals. She is not at this point aware of having something there—a vagina. She is aware only of a lack, an empty and dark hole. This has been her unconscious body-image, which is now surfacing to consciousness.

A distortion of body-image in the genital area is of primary importance to one's sense of identity, and in particular, this very common unconscious self-image of a "hole" in the genital area has a devastating effect on one's sense of value and self-esteem.

It is intriguing that while Sandra unmistakably feels an emptiness and not the presence of anatomical organs in the lower region of her body, she is not out of touch with her body; she is in fact acutely aware of it, much more than is normal for her. This is an important point, because an objection can be raised that what is happening here is that she has no awareness in that particular area of her body—so she feels an emptiness. But it is quite the opposite. It is because her awareness during the experience is acute in this area of her body that she is able to feel an impression of a lack, an empty hole. This impression of a hole has been there all the time as part of an unconscious body-image. Only by working through many resistances has she gained the level of awareness in this area of her body which can lift the repression against this particular part of her body-image.

In a short while, after some cathartic work, the emotional stage subsides and there remains only the experience of an empty hole in the pelvic region. This hole starts expanding to include all the lower belly. She feels and sees a large and empty dark hole. I encourage her to surrender to her experience, to let it unfold. This emptiness, by now a sense of actual emptiness both physical and mental, expands upward to include all her body. She becomes aware of some physical tensions at the throat and diaphragm. By focusing on the tension, she becomes aware of her fear of this experience and starts crying. Crying eliminates the physical tension, and now she feels all of herself as empty and nothing. She experiences that her body has lost its boundaries. This lack of boundaries is exactly what had caused her fear. I encourage her just to observe and not identify with her experience. She feels empty and light, quite airy—as if a light breeze is passing through her. After the fear subsides, her state becomes light, bouncy and expanded. Her sense of herself is spacious and open. It is similar to experiencing the space around her body, but fresh and clear. In fact, there are no boundaries between inside and outside; it all feels the same, a spacious openness. She notices she cannot think the way she usually does, and this brings more fear. Her mind is empty; the usual thoughts do not prevail.

It is important to note here that the main cause of her anxiety is the unexpectedness and the unfamiliarity of the experience of the loss of boundaries, both physical and mental. We can infer this from the fact that when she understands these causes of the anxiety, it subsides, and the experience becomes one of a pleasant spaciousness and a sense of joyful freedom. In fact, in a short time her chest area feels expansive and open, and she feels a warmth, a fine gentleness and a loving kindness.

We see that the sense of spaciousness that results from the dissolution of boundaries is a real, lived experience when the person's capacity for awareness is developed and refined. It is closely connected with the physical body. It is not abstract or metaphorical. It is as real as experiencing one's own body.

In this case, Sandra has experienced, as a result of lifting repressions, the unconscious body-image that is at the core of her self-image. This brought about an experience of expansion in her mind that culminated, after she worked through some body contractions, in such an expanded state that she even felt as if the boundaries of her body were dissolving. She has experienced herself as spaciousness, as openness—in other words, as space. We call it inner space, a parallel to physical space.

The reader might now have many doubts, objections, questions, even anxieties. We will address some of them shortly. But first, we must note here that by dissolving a self-boundary—in this case, the unconscious body-image of being castrated—the person experiences spaciousness or space. We have traveled in our exploration, through the above case history, from the experience of spaciousness to the experience of open space. Space is the intimate experience of the nature of one's mind.

It is not important here to establish the exact ontological status of the phenomenon we are here calling "inner space." We will later refer to many aspects and descriptions of this space from psychoanalytic, Western philosophical, and Eastern spiritual sources. Here, we will describe our own clinical evidence, which is the result of systematic exploration with many individuals. The concept of an actual "inner space" is probably unfamiliar to most readers, because our usual self-image contains an unchallenged belief that we cannot experience space directly, or that there is no such thing as an inner open space. We are here dissolving this boundary, because we have ample evidence both in experience and clinical case studies—evidence that has been repeated and can be duplicated—that the dissolution of a self-boundary invokes the experience of inner open space. Of course, it can be experienced as a form of spaciousness, but we are asserting here that if the awareness is more refined as a result of dissolving more self-boundaries, the experience is definitely and directly of open space—open, empty, and freeing. This is the main insight of our investigation; the following evidence and discussion will support it.

Our evidence suggests that the more the rigid boundaries of the self are made porous and dissolved, the clearer and sharper becomes the experience of the mind as space. The experience of one's self and one's mind as open, pure spaciousness, an empty clear space, becomes increasingly available. The experience is pleasant and freeing, bringing lightheartedness and a clear joy. In the experience of spaciousness and openness, one experiences the absence of emotional heaviness and a release of the sense of burden. There is mental clarity and a lucidity of perception. All the senses become sharper, as if cleansed and rejuvenated. The body feels light, relaxed, agile, and buoyant. It is similar to the experience of being in a clear open space with fresh and crisp air—as if on the top of a high mountain on a clear day, or on a broad beach—but it is experienced inside. And ultimately it becomes clear that we are not a subject experiencing this spaciousness—we are the spaciousness.

The experience of the nature of the mind as space is not new. It has always been known by some, as attested by poets and philosophers. It is the central insight around which some of the major religions, particularly Buddhism, are built. Evans-Wentz, in his translation of a major text of Mahayana Buddhism, says in discussing the mind:

> Of mind per se, concerning which the occident has no clear if any, conception whatsoever, our text teaches: in its true state (of unmodified, unshaped primordialness), mind is naked, immaculate, not made of anything, being of the voidness; clear, vacuous, without duality, transparent; timeless, uncompounded, unimpeded, colorless or devoid of characteristic. (W.Y. Evans-Wentz, *The Tibetan Book of the Great Liberation*, p. 9.)*

Any understanding of the mind as "being of the voidness," as empty space, has great significance and some startling implications for depth psychology, which we will begin to explore as we investigate more specific issues regarding self-image and body-image.

---

* The Buddhist concept of Sunyata (Void) is not identical with the space we are discussing here. However, the two concepts coincide at the deeper levels of space. See Chapter Twenty, in this book.

CHAPTER SEVEN

Self-Image and Body-Image in Relation to Space

Now we turn to some possible questions about and objections to the inferences we draw from the case history of Sandra given in Chapter 6. The reader might object that her experience of space is an isolated example, not necessarily representative of the dissolution of boundaries of body or self-image. On the contrary, our evidence suggests that it happens in all cases of dissolution of self-boundaries; we will explore the dynamics of this process in much greater detail. Another example will be useful here.

Martha is a married, professional woman in her thirties. Her unconscious self-image includes the presence of a penis. This is again a case frequently encountered in psychoanalysis; this type of woman is called a phallic woman.

After months of analyzing her phallic identification, she finally becomes conscious that she believes she has an invisible penis, and that her acting in an aggressive, independent, competitive, and defensive manner is mostly due to this unconscious body-image. The result is that she has lost this identification and has started feeling worthless, inferior, and empty. This is a profound development, with implications for the whole of Martha's life, which she has structured around a strong phallic identification. The phallic identification has given her a sense of who she is, a sense that she has tenaciously defended in all ways available to her. Every challenge to her identification she has naturally felt as an attack. And because such challenges are always present, because of the unrealistic nature of the identification, she has found herself frequently (although to her chagrin) very defensive. Not only was she defending her individuality and independence, but she obviously unconsciously was defending against unconscious, unpleasant affects of the castration ideas that arose. (This should serve to illustrate that the work on understanding the self-image is not an easy endeavor. It is quite an advanced step in self-understanding that requires integrity, perseverance, and sincerity.)

In one session, then, we find Martha starting to experience some somatic changes, tensions and pains in the genital region. In a defensive moment she gets angry and wants to argue with me. I see that she is reverting back to her phallic identification. However, she has already seen through it. So I ask her to sense her pelvic region. She realizes now how she is trying to harden part of that region so that she will feel a penis there. Seeing this, she starts to feel hopeless because she finds only a hole in that area. This is a common transition for the phallic woman. The masculine identification is a denial of reality, the reality of the absence of a penis. But this denial exists only because the absence of a penis is seen as a castration. So when the phallic identification is abandoned, the denial can also be abandoned. Then the woman experiences what she has been denying: the idea of castration and the affects associated with it. In the case of Martha, understanding the phallic identification has actually disposed of the unconscious fantasy of having a penis. Now she is trying to revert back to the older pattern, as happens often in the working through of any psychological conflict, but finds her attempt unsuccessful, thanks to the work of understanding.

It is interesting that the change in the self-image does not focus her attention on the hole in the pelvis, but instead she starts feeling her psychological state changing; she starts feeling mentally more objective and disidentified from her emotions. She also feels a tingling sensation on the top of her head. The state of objectivity develops into the experience of space. She feels pleasantly empty, open, objective, and light. She experiences her head as losing its sense of physical boundaries. She feels the inside of her head as pure space, and after a short while, she feels space inside the rest of the body.

We will see later that the sensation on the top of the head is universally related to the experience of space, and is connected to the shaking of the spine, as in Sandra's case. We will leave these aspects until later when we discuss the phenomenology of space.

The reader might object to the possibility of an actual body-image of a hole in the "castrated" woman. In our experience, phallic identification is always accompanied by an unconscious body-image of having a penis, whereas "castrated" women always have an unconscious body-image of having an empty hole. This phenomenon is documented in psychoanalytic publications. The image of having an empty hole is found to be connected with the feeling these women have of wanting to swallow the man up in sexual intercourse.

The unconscious image of an empty dark hole is not restricted to women. Many men have this unconscious self-image. It is also usually connected with a feeling of castration, of having no penis. Instead of a realistic image of the genitals, the unconscious body-image contains an emptiness, an absence, that is experienced emotionally by both sexes as a sense of castration and deficiency. Men tend to defend against this state more than women, because of their greater emotional reaction to it. We will give other examples of this "genital hole" in case histories in subsequent sections.

Another objection to our findings might be that the cases so far relate only the body-image of an empty hole to the experience of space—that since the experience of an empty hole is very close to the experience of space, perhaps the experience of space is nothing but the experience of a hole that is magnified, or at most, that space can only result from the body-image of a hole. We will answer by citing different kinds of cases.

Kate is a woman in her late twenties who has been working on self-understanding for several years. This work has already led her to the experience of space. Here we find her talking to me about her face. She seems to be fixated on a certain somatic representation of her image. She is feeling physical tension under her eyes and across her nose. This has not happened before. She is obsessed by these sensations but does not know why. Her unconscious body-image is distorted. I ask her to look at her nose in a mirror. She is struck by how different it looks from her mental image of it. Her mental image, which is also felt physically, is that her nose is shorter and more rounded, the way she remembers it when she was a child. Now it is sharper and more pointed.

Here, right at the moment of seeing her unconscious body-image contrasted to the real one, she starts experiencing empty space exactly where the tension is in the face. After a short while, the tension is gone and her face feels normal again, but with a new self-image. This starts a process of remembering certain childhood experiences of sibling rivalry with her sister for mother's attention and related issues about wearing glasses. The body-image of a child's nose had been part of her image as a young girl in rivalry with her sister. The previously unconscious self-image of a little girl has been pushing to enter consciousness because of her work on understanding herself, and came to consciousness through an investigation of its related body-image. The tension on the face, undoubtedly connected with the childhood tension or embarrassment about wearing glasses, was the physical aspect of the defense against this body-image and the affects of memories associated with it.

We see in this example evidence that space is connected not only to the body-image of an empty hole. An image of an empty hole is just one possible distortion of the body-image; the child's nose is a particular distortion of Kate's body-image. We should note here that Kate has a highly developed awareness of her body sensation. Another less sensitive person might go through these changes without being consciously aware of the space. The beginner seldom observes the presence of space, and for beginners the space lasts only for a very short time and does not fully develop into the spacious quality. It goes unnoticed and is not allowed to develop because awareness of it will bring formidable anxieties in the beginner. So it is quickly repressed, and we tend not to point out its presence, because bringing it to the consciousness of the student will only evoke resistances that will make the work more difficult.

Kate's case will be used later to illustrate techniques for imparting the experience of space, and to demonstrate how to use this experience for the psychoanalysis of unconscious complexes.

Having seen that space is connected to the dissolution of body-image boundaries, we might ask how it is connected to the self-image as a whole. Two answers arise. First, according to psychoanalytic object relations theory, body-image actually forms the core of the self-image. The self-image forms as self-representations are gradually built around the experience of the body-image. Margaret Mahler describes this process:

> Pari passu, and in accordance with the pleasure-pain sequences, demarcation of representations of body ego within the symbiotic matrix takes place. These representations are deposited as the "body image" (Schilder, 1923; Mahler & Furer, 1966). . . . The body ego contains two kinds of self-representation: an inner core of the body-image, with a boundary that is turned toward the inside of the body and divides it from the ego, and an outer layer of sensoriperceptive engrams that contributes to the boundaries of the "body self" (cf. Bergmar, 1963, discussing Federn's concepts). . . .
>
> The infant's inner sensations form the core of the self. They seem to remain the central crystallization point of the "feeling of self," around which a "sense of identity" will become established (Greenacre, 1958; Mahler, 1958b, Rose, 1964, 1966). The sensoriperceptive

organ—the "peripheral rind of the ego," as Freud called it—contributes mainly to the self's demarcation from the object world. The two kinds of intra-psychic structures together form the framework for self-orientation (Spiegel, 1959). (Margaret Mahler, et al., *The Psychological Birth of the Human Infant*, pp. 46-47.)

The second answer to the question of how space is connected to the self-image as a whole is illustrated in the following case history.

Larry is a married man in his early thirties. In a group setting he is asking me to help him understand an aspect of his relationship to his wife. I point out to him that he is talking to me in a flat voice that doesn't reflect the content of his question. He feels cut off emotionally and doesn't experience much sensation in his body. I point out that he is always like this when he talks to me. He becomes aware of a knot in his solar plexus. Increasing his awareness of the character structure he is presenting, he is struck by how much it sounds like his father. He mentions how he always thought he was not like his father and never wanted to be like him in any way. In other words, he is now becoming conscious of his identification with his father—the defended-against self-image, in this case, of a passive, feminine man.

He then starts experiencing tingling sensations on the top of the head, and along with this sensation, the inner experience of space. The head sensations are very definite; in fact, another group member, Sandra, becomes aware of them through empathic identification which, interestingly enough, starts the experience of shaking in her. This case study illustrates how space is connected with self-image and not restricted to the narrower concept of body-image.

CHAPTER EIGHT

Inner Space and Spatial Extension

I nner space is, of course, not the usual physical space, and is not tied only to body images. It is affected by self-boundaries that are more emotional and psychological in nature, as illustrated in Larry's case in the previous chapter. There is a correspondence on the ontological level to the relation between the self-image and the body-image. In other words, just as self-image includes body-image in object relations theory, so in the experience of space, inner psychological space includes the notion of space as spatial extension. Inner space is not restricted to spatial extension, just as self-image is not restricted to body-image, which is analogous to spatial extension.

Here we can appreciate how the findings of object relations theory regarding the relationship between self-image and body-image help us to understand more clearly the concept of inner space, and to extend our insight into the nature of the mind as space. This inner space is bigger, more open, more encompassing than the notion of space as spatial extension. Focusing on the dissolution of the boundaries of the body-image, which are mental analogues of physical boundaries, tends to prejudice us towards seeing space as spatial extension. But dissolving these boundaries, which are mental in nature, helps us open the experience of space to other dimensions that are more psychological. We see that spatial openness is only one dimension in inner space.

We will show later that by deepening our understanding of inner space, and by finding in it more dimensions of openness, we will be able to expand our knowledge of object relations and gain more insight into the psychic structure. In particular, we will be able to explore on a more fundamental level the nature of identity, of the self, and its relation to self-image. We will be able to extend the findings of object relations theory to an understanding of the ontological nature of the ego, a question that has not yet been approached in traditional psychoanalysis.

This notion of space as openness in more dimensions than the spatial will help us to construct a theory about inner space and self-image. First, however, we must say more about this new notion of space. As the experience of space repeats, deepens, and expands in the gradual process of dissolving self-boundaries, the individual becomes aware of more subtle kinds of boundaries. He becomes aware of and can dissolve boundaries regarding the depth and extent of his feelings, the kinds and types of feelings and sensations he can have, the extent of his awareness of both mind and body, and the categories of possible experiences of himself and the world.

Space brings about expansion in the qualities of our senses, our sensations, and our mental capacities. It deepens our intuition. It expands our awareness into new dimensions of ourselves, some we would never have conceived could exist. It brings new capacities for perception and experience. In addition, space has the surprising and powerful capacity of expanding itself, continuously increasing the openness and dissolution of boundaries, allowing ever-greater understanding of ourselves and our minds.

CHAPTER NINE

Self-Image as the Structuralization of Space

We have seen so far that awareness of the self-image brings about the experience of space, or of the mind as openness. In other words, dissolution of boundaries imposed by the self frees space. It literally expands the mind. Understanding this dynamic relation between self-image and space, we can theorize about the development of psychic structure: The development of the self-image simply represents a gradual building and structuralization of boundaries in the mind space.

Here we see the relationship between mind as content and mind as ground. Space is mind as ground. Mind as content is a result of boundaries in this space. In fact, these boundaries are the mind as content, are what constitutes the psychic structure.

The neonate is born with no boundaries in its mind space, i.e., with no psychic structure. Its mind is just space, openness with no boundaries, physical or mental. This assumption is consistent with the notion of the undifferentiated matrix in object relations theory (Hartmann), with some difference: The absence of boundaries in the neonatal matrix is usually considered a state of non-differentiation, whereas our perspective sees the matrix as the lack of boundaries.

> Hartmann's postulate is that the neonate is equipped with an undifferentiated matrix with which there exist apparatuses of primary autonomy. After ego and id differentiate, these will serve ego. There is, therefore, an implied existence of an innate ego constitution as well as other innate factors which come into play after differentiation. (Gertrude R. and Rubin Blanck, *Ego Psychology, Theory & Practice*, p. 37.)

The concept of the undifferentiated matrix is later enlarged to denote the lack of differentiation between, and the existence of, the constitutional factors that later differentiate into, the ego, id, and superego. Thus the psychic structure exists only in potential form for the neonate.

However, the emphasis is obviously on the absence of boundaries in the sense of absence of differentiation, i.e., differentiation is seen as the development of boundaries. The undifferentiated matrix is characterized by a lack of differentiation between its various contents: between inner and outer, pleasant and painful, mind and body, libido and aggression, self and other, and so on. The development of the psychic structure and hence of the self-image is seen as a process of structuralization of the mind. In fact, object relations theory is primarily an understanding of how this structure develops out of an undifferentiated state of the mind. Gertrude and Rubin Blanck, who have attempted to synthesize the findings of ego psychology, have put it thus:

> . . . the basic assumption of developmental theory is that the experience (the resultant of interaction between the innate and the surround) must become "metabolized" to form structure. Fleming (personal communication) suggests that such process precedes

organization. In this analogy the products of the interaction consist of small mobile units which lend themselves to organization into more complex units with
stable structure. (Gertrude R. and Rubin Blanck, *Ego
Psychology II*, p. 11.)

Given our understanding of mind as space, we can see then
that the separation-individuation process that Mahler speaks of not
only builds the psychic structure and gives the individual his
sense of identity, but more fundamentally, it accomplishes this by
erecting boundaries and fixing them in space. In other words, the
process of ego development is a process of bounding space, of
building static boundaries in the openness of the mind. It is the
carving of structure out of space, and the resulting psychic structure then is simply a structuralized space. This explains very
clearly why when self-boundaries are dissolved, space appears.
What happens is that the structuralization is dissolved, the boundaries are "melted." When the structure is melted, the nature of the
mind with no structure is revealed, and this is space.

Although this interpretation may seem to indicate a departure
from the realm of ego psychology and a movement toward the
Eastern notions which include the idea of mind as space as a com-
monplace understanding, we must note here that our interpretation does not conflict in any way with the findings of object
relations theory and ego psychology in general. In fact, it clarifies the process of development and sharpens our understanding of the undifferentiated matrix. We see that the undifferentiated
matrix not only lacks differentiation, it also lacks limitations. The
neonate has no sense of limitation; in fact, ego psychology has
found that for some time the child has no sense of the limitation
of his capacities.

This phenomenon is acutely manifested in the second subphase of the separation-individuation process, what is called the
practicing subphase. It manifests as a sense of magical omnipo-
tence, of grandiosity, of imperviousness to physical hurt, of obliv-
iousness to boundaries and limitations. This is accompanied by a
feeling of joy and elation. Mahler describes this phase thus:

> . . . and the child seems intoxicated with his own faculties and with the greatness of his own world. Narcissism is at its peak. . . . Along with this, we see a relatively great imperviousness to knocks and falls and other frustrations. . . . He is exhilarated by his own capabilities, continually delighted with the discoveries he makes in his expanding world, and quasi-enamored with the world and his own grandeur and omnipotence. (Margaret Mahler, *et al., op. cit.,* p. 17.)

It is interesting that the practicing period is, for the toddler, an experience of expansion and joy, just as in the course of the rediscovery and experience of space. It is also interesting that some of the qualities of the undifferentiated matrix are identical with those of space: for instance, the absence of differentiation between inner and outer and between mind and body. However, we are not suggesting here that the neonate experiences itself as space in the same way an adult experiences his mind as space; we are only pointing out the qualities of spaciousness and openness in the concept of the undifferentiated matrix.* Most likely, the perceptual apparatus of the neonate is not developed enough to experience the undifferentiated matrix as space. (We must note here that the severe object anxiety that is experienced when the psychic structure threatens to collapse, or in the severely nondifferentiated state of some psychotic and borderline individuals, is not due to the experience of space with no boundaries, but rather to the weakness and insecurity of the boundaries of the psychic structures, or whatever remains of them. In other words, there has to be some psychic structure present for there to be object anxiety, the fear of disintegration. So in the process of dissolving boundaries, the individual might very well encounter object anxiety. Thus the procedure must be conducted in a way that makes this anxiety tolerable, paying attention to the considerations of tact, timing, and the ego of the student.)

---

* We will see later, when we discuss essence or Being, that the inner experience consists of more than mind, and hence more than space. We cannot make a one-to-one correspondence between the undifferentiated matrix and space or any other essential state, because space and essence are actual experience and the undifferentiated matrix is a concept formulated to aid understanding.

CHAPTER TEN

The Psychodynamic Approach to Space

We have demonstrated that ego psychology, or what is specifically called object relations theory, contains the understanding of how the psychic structure is carved out of space, that is, out of openness and unboundedness. Object relations theory provides a clear understanding of how the ego and the sense of identity develop out of the undifferentiated matrix of the neonate by the acquisition of self-boundaries via the process of separation-individuation. The reader who is interested in more detail should consult the many good publications in ego psychology. Our concern here is to demonstrate the relationship between the self-image and space, and to show how the knowledge of ego psychology can be used for reaching the experience of space.

Lacking our present psychoanalytic understanding of the formation and development of ego and identity, none of the old systems which studied the mind were able to investigate its onto-logical nature from a psychodynamic perspective, as we are doing here. Some of those systems, especially the Buddhist one, had worked out a detailed understanding of how the ego is built, or more accurately, how it exists minute to minute as a separate struc-ture. Buddhist meditation techniques lead the practitioner toward a direct, experiential knowledge of the nature of mind as space. This understanding, contained in the Abhidharma and used in Mahayana Buddhism, sees the ego as a certain structure that is maintained in the openness of space. The focus is on the exis-tential process of ego separateness. In the words of Trungpa Rinpoche, a Tibetan Lama,

> Fundamentally there is just open space, the basic ground, what we really are. Our most fundamental state of mind, before the creation of the ego, is such that there is a basic openness, basic freedom, a spacious quality; and we have now and always had this openness. . . . the confused mind is inclined to view itself as a solid on-going thing, but it is only a collection of tendencies, events. (Chogyam Trungpa, *Cutting Through Spiritual Materialism*, pp. 124-125.)

In Buddhist terminology, this collection is referred to as the five Skandhas, or Five Heaps. Trungpa goes on to describe how the heaps develop:

> Having noticed that one is separated, then there is the feeling that one has always been so. It is an awk-wardness, the instinct toward self-consciousness. It is also one's excuse for remaining separate, an individual grain of sand. . . . It is the attitude that one is a con-fused and separate individual, and that is all there is to it. One has identified oneself as separate from the basic landscape of space and openness. (*Ibid.*, pp. 124-125.)

Again we see both the contrast and the connection with object relations theory which focuses on the formation and maintenance of ego as a separate psychic structure. Our case histories show

how the understanding of this theory begins providing a Western contribution to the traditionally spiritual and mystical concern of understanding the nature of the mind.

We see here the beginning of a possible real science of the mind. We have available for the first time both the knowledge of space and the knowledge of the development of psychic structure and sense of identity. We propose not only a comparison or a relationship between the two fields, but a fundamental marriage, a real merging. We see this development not only as a marriage, but as a natural development of the science of the mind.

How do the concepts and practices of psychology relate to our investigation of the relationship of self-image, mind, and space?

All forms of psychotherapy can be seen as a process of altering or modifying the patient's self-image. The particular boundaries of the self that contribute to pathology are recognized, then dissolved or modified to suit a more positive or "healthy" self-image. In the psychodynamic therapies, such as psychoanalysis, those pathological segments of the self-image are brought to consciousness through psychodynamic understanding of their genesis so that the person can test them against "reality." In this way, the pathological segments are either dissolved or modified according to the demands of this "reality." The final outcome is a modified self-image, usually a more expanded one, that allows more choice in experience and action, and hence less suffering.

What interests us here is to see that psychotherapy is largely a process of expanding the self-image, which in our perspective means more openness and spaciousness in the mind. But since the mind is ultimately open and empty space, the process is actually the freeing of more space. The focus of psychotherapy, however, is in the modification of self-image in ways that allow the individual to function in a more tolerable and satisfying state of emotional health, a state called the normal condition. Through this process psychotherapy has helped many people suffering from emotional and mental distress. What if we go beyond this limit of trying to achieve a "normal" condition, if in fact we continue the process of working on the self-image starting with the normal person, the average healthy individual who already functions in a normal state? Working with such a person, who might be motivated to pursue such a process by an intuition of a deeper or truer state of being, we can continue bringing to consciousness elements of the self-image to be checked with "reality," and allowing them to be modified or dissolved to encompass more "reality." Through this process, the person's experience of himself becomes more and more open and spacious until this openness culminates in the direct experience of the nature of the mind: space. It is a gradual process of thawing the frozen boundaries of the ego identity and liberating more and more space. The theory and techniques of psychoanalysis and the various therapies are used here not for the treatment of psychopathology, but for the understanding of the nature of the mind.

CHAPTER ELEVEN

Discussion of Technique

We have shown in our case histories some examples of this process. These examples are mostly representative of individuals who have been involved in this process of understanding for some time. At the beginning it is difficult for the individual to consciously experience space, because the usual experience of oneself is so dense, crowded, and hemmed in, due to the many emotional conflicts and inaccurate beliefs about reality. This is true even for the average or normal person, a fact appreciated only when the person has had his first direct experience of space. As the individual understands himself more—in the process of resolving many emotional conflicts and dissolving many boundaries—his awareness develops and becomes refined. This gradual process of creating more openness and refining one's awareness eventually produces the direct experience of space. Then, continued understanding will dissolve more boundaries at more subtle levels, and hence deepen and expand the experience of space.

Analysts familiar with object relations theory know that at any moment of the therapeutic relationship, a certain unit of object relations is operating. According to Kernberg:

> While therefore the consolidation of the overall intrapsychic structures (ego, superego, and id) results in an integration of internalized object relations that fuses the constituent units within the overall structures, in the course of the psychoanalysis one observes the gradual redissolution of pathogenic superego and ego structures, and, in this context, the activation and clarification of the constituent internalized object relations in the transference. In this regard, Glover's (1955) classical formulation of the transference as reflecting an impulse and an identification may easily be translated into the transference as always reflecting an object relation under the impact of a certain drive derivative. (Harold P. Blum, *Psychoanalytic Exploration of Techniques*, p. 210.)

This means that at any point, the transference consists of a self-image, an object-image (in this case projected on the analyst), and an affect between the two. A unit of object relations is revived from the past and transferred onto the present relationship.

However, at the beginning of the therapeutic process, the focus will naturally be on the overall self-image and the overall projected image—generally the superego seen in the person of the analyst. So the overall self-image and the overall superego are usually analyzed first in a general way, the analysis proceeding to increasingly specific object relations as the process deepens. Both the self-image and the projected image are understood psychodynamically and genetically. Usually the process of psychotherapy focuses more on the affect in the object relation unit, which is usually called the transference feeling. Our methods here focus more on the self-image, so that more boundaries are dissolved and more space is liberated. This usually happens only implicitly in the process of psychotherapy.

As the process deepens, the individual becomes aware of smaller and more specific units of object relations:

> The transference is expressed more and more directly by means of a certain object relation which is used defensively against an opposing one reflecting the repressed drive derivatives. In the case of both defense and impulse determined object relations, the patient may re-enact the self-representation of that unit while projecting the object representation onto the analyst or, at other times, project his self-representation onto the analyst while identifying with the object representation of the unit. (*Ibid.*, p. 211.)

As the ego structure is analyzed more specifically by bringing to consciousness the various identifications that form the units of self-representation, the process goes deeper into the core of the sense of identity, the body image. The deeper aspects of the unconscious body image are brought to consciousness and the affective experiences involved with them understood. As we have seen, object relations theory holds that the core of the sense of separate identity or self-image is the primitive body image formed in the symbiotic state in the first ten months of life. Deeper still, the forerunners of self-representation are revealed, what are called the "not yet differentiated self-object representation," the memory traces of pleasurable and unpleasurable experiences in the merged stage of the symbiotic phase. According to Kernberg, who proposes four stages of the process of structuralization:

> At the second stage, consolidation of the undifferentiated self-object image takes place and is normally libidinally gratifying. This leads to the establishment of a primary intrapsychic structure with memory traces carrying a positive affective charge. Simultaneously, out of the painful and frustrating psychophysiological experiences, a separate structure is built, representing an undifferentiated, "all bad" self-object representation. Thus there arises an "all good" self-object, separate from the "all bad" self-object, with, as yet no separation between self and nonself and only rudimentary ego boundaries. (Gertrude R. and Rubin Blanck, *Ego Psychology: Theory and Practice*, p. 75.)

This last step concerning the merged self-object images is very important for the deepest aspects of the work of self-understanding. If the individual is not aware of the presence of the merged images that are either "all good" or "all bad," as happens in such deep regression, then there might arise much confusion or anxiety. The deepening experience of space is bound to reach such deep recesses of the mind, since it will ultimately, if pursued completely, uncover all repressed content of the unconscious.

As the various elements of self-representations arise to consciousness and are analyzed and understood, the experience of space becomes more frequent. Normally, the experience of space is most easily available through the understanding and correction of body-image, especially the sexual body image, as we have shown in many of our examples.

This is due to many factors:

i. Distorted body-image is frequent and has obvious painful emotional consequences.

ii. Distorted sexual body-image is the most frequent and the most distressing in terms of consequences.

iii. When an unconscious distorted body-image is revealed to consciousness, it is easy to check it against reality, for reality in this case is the actual body of the individual. This is in contrast to the psychological self-image, which is usually much harder to check against "reality" because "reality" in this case is not as defined and clear as the physical body.

iv. In studying body-image, the individual is already acutely aware of spatial extension and hence becomes easily aware of space in its dimension as a spatial openness.

v. As we will see later, much of the defensive structure is an attempt to fill or repress the genital hole, which we mentioned in some of the case histories. This self-image of an empty dark hole occurs in both men and women. From one perspective it is a state of castration; from another, deeper perspective it is experienced as a deficient and empty state of the self. We will show later that both perspectives function as a unity, although the perspective of genital castration surfaces first. The castration perspective is operative in the process of experiencing space through analyzing the sexual body-image, because understanding the genital hole leads directly and smoothly to the experience of space.

vi. Superego analysis can lead to space through bringing the genital hole to awareness. As Kernberg says in the passage quoted above, it is the superego that is usually first encountered in the transference. Continued analysis and psychodynamic understanding of the superego in its various representations will ultimately lead to the main pillar of this part of the psychic structure, namely the castration complex. According to Freud, the superego is developed mainly to repress the Oedipus complex which in turn is due to castration anxiety:

> The superego is, however, not simply a residue of the earliest object choices of the id; it also represents an energetic reaction formation against those choices. Its relation to the ego is not exhausted by the precept: "You ought to be like this (like your father)." It also comprises the prohibition: "You may not do all that he does; some things are his prerogative." This double aspect of the ego ideal had the task of repressing the Oedipus complex; indeed, it is to that revolutionary event that it owes its existence. (S. Freud, *The Ego and the Id*, p. 24.)

The superego, then, is seen to be the heir of the castration fear. So working on the superego, by analysis or otherwise, will ultimately bring to light the Oedipus complex, and with it the issue of castration. Dealing with this issue, and particularly allowing the sense of castration itself to surface into consciousness, will automatically precipitate the experience of the genital hole.

However, it often happens that a person becomes aware of the presence of space before dealing with such deep aspects of body-image. Sometimes this awareness develops in dealing with more superficial layers of body-image, as in the case of Kate. In these cases, it is either as a result of deep cathartic experiences or greater refinement of the perceptual faculty. In addition, there are cases where the student becomes aware of the presence of space as a result of empathic identification with another person who happens to be experiencing space.

In psychodynamic technique, we follow the general rule of first analyzing resistance and then the actual material defended against. Kernberg's insight that even defense or resistance comprises an object relation is very useful in our technique of understanding self-image:

> Unconscious intrapsychic conflicts are never simple conflicts between impulse and defense; rather, the drive derivative finds expression through a certain primitive object relation (a certain unit of self- and object-representation); and the defense, too, is reflected by a certain internalized object relation. The conflict is between these intrapsychic structures. Thus, all character defenses really reflect the activation of a defensive constellation of self- and object-representations directed against an opposite and dreaded repressed self- and object-constellation. (Harold P. Blum, *op. cit.*, p. 210.)

In Larry's case (p. 29), resistance is what I really interpreted to him. The object relation consisted of his image of himself as a passive and castrated young boy, and his image of me, that of a big and knowing authoritative father. The affect was of fear and timidity. The interpretation of this object relation made him aware of the repressed unit, which is the image of himself as an angry and rebellious child, of me as a cruel castrating father, and of the affect of murderous rage. In the process of becoming aware of the self-image which was involved in his resistance and comparing this with his conscious self-image, space manifested. Space then dissolved or erased his defensive self-image, allowing to emerge the defended-against image of the rebellious and angry child, an aspect of his character I had seen for some time, but which he could not acknowledge until this time. This self-image is one part of the triad of the repressed object relation unit. With it, of course, manifested the projected object image, that of the castrating father, and the affect of rage. Understanding this object relation precipitated the activation of the whole oedipal situation. Here we clearly see the technique of using the understanding of self-image for encouraging the experience of space, and we also see how space dissolves the boundaries of the self, thereby dissolving defenses and deepening the process of understanding.

When we speak of defenses or self-images dissolving during a session, we clearly don't claim that a given boundary or image dissolves permanently upon being brought to awareness, even when a deep experience of space results. As in many therapeutic processes, the process is much more complex. It involves reactions of anxiety to the expansion taking place, habitual responses to demands from the environment which are based on the old self-images, and resistance to the arising of ever deeper layers of object relations units, as well as the positive affects associated with the sense of expansion and the intrinsically satisfying experiences of insight.

Our evidence suggests that when the conscious self-image is seen in comparison with the surfacing unconscious self-image, space arises spontaneously. If the individual holds both images in his mind, he will see (or feel) empty space appearing and both images dissolving. For some time there will be only empty space. Then an image reappears. Which image is left depends on whether the self-image investigated is psychological or body-image.

We see, therefore, that the experience of space corrects the distortions of body-image. The perception of the body, both from outside and inside, becomes objective. Space seems to allow objective perception. In terms of physical reality, it removes distortion. This is the reason that when an individual experiences space while retaining unconscious distortions of body-image, distortions in the perception of physical reality result that are sometimes experienced as spatial hallucinations or disturbances in the perception of body balance. We believe these distortions can be analyzed and seen as the result of body-image distortions pushing toward consciousness, but compounded with the effects of defenses against them. Some experience their bodies as twisted one way or another, or experience a distortion in the proportions of different parts of the body, or experience their posture as different from what it is. What is really happening in those instances—and they do occur in sessions of psychotherapy, especially in body-oriented therapies—is a readjustment in the self-image that is only partially conscious. These distortions of body-image happen in the beginning experience of space, when the person is still burdened with many unconscious distortions in body-image and the affects associated with them. What actually happens is that the appearance of space challenges and brings to consciousness the various unconscious distortions of body-image all at once. But the individual, for reasons of defense, cannot tolerate seeing all these distortions, so he experiences only a sense of distortion or disorientation that is not specific enough to clarify the self-image or the affective components associated with the specific distortions.

This kind of disorientation happened to Kate in her first conscious encounter with space. She was at home with her parents and, for reasons connected with her work on understanding herself, space arose in her consciousness. She didn't see it as space, neither did she understand what was happening. She just suddenly started feeling somewhat dizzy and nauseated. She felt disoriented in space, as if she couldn't walk or balance herself as she stood. Her perception of her body and physical environment were distorted and changing. This naturally produced anxiety. After she calmed down somewhat, she called me on the phone. I knew immediately she was experiencing space, but I asked her some questions about her experience to find out what caused the distortions. It turned out that she had most recently been paying attention to issues concerning her gender identity in relation to her body-image. When she saw some of the issues and conflicts around her sexual identity, her state became more balanced. She became aware of space pervading her. This made very clear to her the various identifications affecting her gender identity, and started a deep process of working through these identifications and the affects around them. We see here, then, that Kate's understanding of the distortions in her body-image, her disorientation and distortion of perception led quickly to the perception of space. In cases where the self-image investigated is psychological, then the arising of space will still bring, as in the case of body-image, the affective experiences associated with the unconscious self-image.

This illustrates the primary reason for the extreme difficulty encountered when an individual attempts to achieve a clear experience of open space through meditation techniques, as in Eastern spiritual schools; for the experience of space, because it involves the dissolving of defenses, will bring into consciousness any distortions in body-image. The defense mechanisms of the ego will then automatically mobilize to prevent consciousness of the affective experiences associated with these distortions. This mobilization of defenses in effect amounts to the repression of space. Space not only reveals distortions, but because it exposes self-boundaries, it naturally brings into consciousness all the identifications making up these boundaries, as well as any affects and memories connected to them. Naturally then, space will be vehemently defended against. Space is actually dynamically repressed; and this fact, besides explaining the difficulty in experiencing space, indicates the usefulness of psychodynamic techniques to those seeking this experience. Our experience is that the psychodynamic method does allow greater success than simple meditation in eliciting the perception of space, especially when it is used in understanding and eliminating the difficulties that arise in response to the experience of space.

A crucial aspect of our technique is holding both images—the conscious self-image and the newly arising unconscious self-image—simultaneously in one's attention for the space to appear and for the affects to become conscious. Evidence suggests that if the person becomes aware of a previously unconscious self-image without contrasting it with the conscious one, not much happens, or rather, resistances against affects seem to stay in force. An example will illustrate this point further.

Anna, a married woman whom I have been working with for three years, is telling me that she has been feeling angry at men recently. I interpret her actions and expression by pointing out to her that she seems to have an attitude of being a dependent little girl with those big adult men. (We should note here that there is no absolute distinction between body-images and more psychological ones. The constellation of Anna's little-girl images clearly includes both.) She is struck by how true this is, and admits that this is not the image she usually has of herself. Her affective state does not change much, except for disliking the new information and mildly resenting me for it. I suggest that she consider both the image of the little girl and the image she likes of herself. I do this because I see that she is unconsciously identifying with the little girl image and that this identification is too close for her to feel her affects or to see that she is transferring to me from this self-image. This instantly invokes space, and she breaks down sobbing with tremendous hurt and begins yelling with murderous rage at her father. Understanding these feelings changes them to soft crying as she realizes how much she loved and adored her big father.

So it seems at first that space has the capacity to erase resistance, which in Anna represented a certain boundary. Second, space arises not as a result of becoming aware of a certain unconscious self-image, but as the result of seeing the difference between it and the conscious self-image. The contrast or contradiction between the two images evokes the presence of space, which then goes about erasing them, leaving only the experience of open space. This process also frees the affective components.

We return now to the case of the psychological self-image and the associated affects. As these affects and memories are worked through psychodynamically, this self-image is accordingly modified. Usually, the self-image includes a physical counterpart because each psychological distortion is accompanied by a physical distortion, usually as physical tension patterns, which Wilhelm Reich called the body armor: "In character-analytic practice, we discover the armor functioning in the form of a chronic, frozen, muscular-like bearing." (Wilhelm Reich, *Character Analysis*, p. 337.) As the self-image is modified, the physical distortion is corrected, i.e., the physical tension is dissolved. Larry, in the case presented in Chapter 7, had a knot in his solar plexus. When he worked through the affects related to the image, the tension dissolved and the knot disappeared. He started feeling lighter and more relaxed. The presence of space produced a sense of emotional balance and openness.

When issues around a given self-image are worked through the next object relation unit usually surfaces, with its own specific self-image. In Larry's case, for a few weeks after the session, he manifested more and more the self-image of the rebellious and angry child. The work continues by understanding this object relation and dissolving its image, allowing the next object relation to emerge. This continues, going deeper into the person's identifications. This is different from the case of the body-image, where there is an end—the actual, accurate image of the physical body. In terms of the sense of identity, there is no objective and ontologically real self-image where the individual can end in this process of dissolving boundaries. Rather, when he persists in psychodynamic understanding of his mind, the experience of space becomes more frequent until it becomes a permanently available condition. The boundaries continue to dissolve, revealing more and more space. Every arising self-image indicates the presence of boundaries which can then be dissolved by space.

We see here very clearly that self-image bounds and binds space. We also see that expansion of self-boundaries can be a continuing process with no limits. Ultimately, even the experience of space is divested of its boundaries, i.e., the boundary of space defined as an experience—or even the boundary of the *notion* of no boundaries. This is what Tarthang Tulku calls Great Space:

> Eventually, we can discover a space that involves no concepts at all, since concepts are simply indications of the relative capacity and resistance of a particular space. . . . The accommodating quality which is represented at its peak by Great Space is complete at precisely the point where the notion of a space, which to a greater or lesser degree allows or accommodates a "thing," collapses. The openness and allowing qualities of Great Space are greatest when not filtered through a "thing which allows". . . While there "are" partitioning concepts and distinctions within lower spaces, there "are not" such distinctions at the level of Great Space, and

also "no" isolated Great Space. (Tarthang Tulku, *Time, Space and Knowledge*, pp. 14–16.)

We see here that Tarthang, in his discussion of space, regards boundaries both as bounding surfaces, as we do, and also as partitioning surfaces. In fact, space can be regarded as the absence of partitioning boundaries, as Tarthang Tulku sees it, and hence also as an absence of differentiation. This sheds more light on our previous discussion of space as it relates to Hartmann's concept of the "undifferentiated matrix" and clarifies how structure development from the matrix is a structuralization of space through differentiation.

Not only does space correct the distortion of body-image and dissolve the psychological boundaries of the self-image, it ultimately dissolves the self-image as a rigid structure bounding experience. This provides a hint regarding the ontological truth about self-image. Since we see that space makes the body-image objective and realistic, i.e., correcting it according to objective reality, we can assume that it also corrects the self-image according to objective reality. That is, ontologically, self-image is simply boundaries frozen in space, frozen by their cathexis with libidinal energy. When the cathexis is undone, the boundaries dissolve into empty space, which is what actually exists as the nature of the mind. Therefore, we can say that pursuing psychodynamic understanding of the self-image all the way to the end will leave us with, among other things, a real and objective body-image and the experience of the mind as open space.

What happens, then, to the functioning ego, when a person goes though this process? We address this question in Chapter 13, "Space and Essence." Here it suffices to say that the ego identity becomes increasingly "transparent"; the person's experience depends less and less on unconscious self-images and object relations units. Thus the person comes into clearer, more objective contact with the environment, and as the experience of space is allowed, there arises naturally within that space a clear, full presence, which without the rigidity and defensiveness of ego can assume ego's functions in a vastly more mature, objective and deeply fulfilling manner.

We have shown so far how psychodynamic understanding of self-image leads to the experience of space, and how space, in turn, by modifying or erasing self-image, brings forth the unconscious affects and memories. However, this is not the main action or usefulness of space in this process. As we have seen, the main characteristics of space are openness and the absence of rigid boundaries. It is precisely these characteristics that make it most useful; for when space is present, it acts by challenging and exposing the unconscious self-boundaries of the individual. Since its nature is the absence of boundaries, it will naturally challenge any existing boundaries. This challenge usually manifests as anxiety, because the exposure of unconscious self-boundaries actually lifts certain repressions, and the possibility of lifting any repression arouses anxiety. This is because repression is a response to anxiety: ". . . it is the attitude of anxiety on the part of the ego which is the motive of and the incitement to repression." (Sigmund Freud, *The Problem of Anxiety*, p. 40.) So when repression is being challenged, we are first confronted with anxiety. But this anxiety is what is called signal anxiety, the fear that signals the presence of danger and hence brings about repression, i.e., the removal of the perception of danger from consciousness.

However, in the deeper experiences of space another kind of anxiety becomes more important—what is called object anxiety, the fear of disintegration or of losing one's sense of identity. This is understandable since space erases boundaries, some of which make up the self-image which forms the sense of ego identity. So space is really experienced as a threat to the ego. In fact it is a threat to a rigid and frozen ego that needs its territory, boundaries, and separateness in order to be defended.

Pamela is a woman in her mid-twenties. She is talking to me in a group training session, and she is in an emotionally receptive and mentally open state. I am explaining a certain aspect of theory, but I happen to be experiencing space as I am talking. By empathic identification she starts experiencing the space consciously for the first time. She feels somewhat disoriented, "spaced out." I ask her if there is anything in her experience that is unpleasant. She says no, but that she feels scared because she can't think. Her mind is empty. I ask her what's so scary about not thinking. She realizes it is because she believes she won't know who she is because she is usually always thinking. This understanding comforts her somewhat, but doesn't totally dispel the anxiety. This experience starts her on a few months exploration of her affects surrounding the issues of symbiotic merger and separation-individuation.

This case also illustrates certain phenomena regarding boundaries and body image. First, we have shown that challenging boundaries can bring awareness to distortions in the perception of the physical body. More important, the boundaries are seen to exist as certain patterns of physical tension in segments of the body armor.

We should remember here our original purpose in investigating space: besides challenging boundaries, the experience of space leads us toward understanding the nature of the mind. In Chapter 13, we will discuss how the experience and knowledge of space are also useful as entries into the knowledge and experience of Being or essence. First we will go more deeply into the phenomenology of space, by investigating the various ways it actually manifests.

CHAPTER TWELVE

Phenomenology of Space

We have described some of the somatic manifestations that accompany the appearance of space in consciousness, such as sensations on the top of the head and shaking in the body, specifically shaking of the spinal column. For most people the first sign that space is manifesting is the awareness of some definite sensation on the top of the head. It feels like a gentle tingling, or sometimes, as if something is brushing against one's hair. If the person is ready for the experience, it will develop into more intense sensations at the top of the head which can sometimes feel painful. This will develop into the distinct physical impression of the presence of a hole on the top of the head, as if part of the cranium is missing. This is usually a gentle and pleasant impression, quite distinct and unmistakable.

Lara is a woman in her mid-thirties, married with children, and at this time she is talking to me in a Work group setting. We are discussing her belief that it is bad or objectionable for her to be happy and joyful in a childlike, playful manner. I am aware that she is at the moment experiencing a lot of joy and delight, but she is reporting painful feelings. As she explores her defensive image of the suffering woman, she becomes aware of the joy she is actually feeling; she feels it pervading her chest. At this point she starts becoming aware of a tingling sensation at the top of her head. By focusing on it, she becomes aware of a specific impression of a hole or opening on the top of her head around the anterior fontanel. I don't pursue this experience with her, partially because she is just experiencing a new expansion (joy), and partially because I know she has many fears about losing her sense of identity, fears that go along with a defensive stubbornness in thinking furiously and being in her head.

What is actually happening in the experience of the hole is that the individual consciousness is in tune with the dimension of space in that area of the head. Since space is experienced as nothing, there is the impression of a hole in the cranium, as if the top of the head has been surgically removed. This is not a hallucination; it is an actual accurate perception of the dimension of space localized in that area.

If the person is more sensitive, then he will be aware that the hole is really a part of a column of space which starts at the cranium and goes upward into the space above. This perception is good evidence that the space we are discussing is not the common physical space, since it can be differentiated from physical space by a fine perceptual capacity. Also, more refined perception can sense the onset of the experience of space as a descent of a column of empty space above the head. When it impinges on the cranium, the individual has an impression of a hole.

This experience, if the person is not too frightened and is ready for it, will automatically develop as the perception of a column of space extending downward in the head. Now the person will be aware of it more definitively as an empty space, instead of as a hole. The mind is experienced as clear, empty and lucid.

This experience was seen by Sri Aurobindo, the Indian teacher and founder of Integral Yoga, as the definitive necessary beginning of his yoga and teaching. The space in the head is experienced as the absence of content in the mind, as a peaceful silence. In a letter, Aurobindo writes:

> I find nothing to object to Prof. Sarley's comment on the still, bright and clear mind; for it adequately indicates the process by which the mind makes itself ready for the reflection of the higher truth in its undisturbed surface or substance. One thing perhaps needs to be kept in view—this pure stillness of the mind is always the required condition, the desideratum, but to bring it about there are more ways than one.
>
> It can happen also by a descent from above of a great spiritual stillness imposing silence on the mind and heart and the life stimuli and the physical reflexes. (Sri Aurobindo, *On Himself,* pp. 84-85.)

The column of space can descend all the way down into the body, encompassing the spinal column. This can cause shaking in the spine or in the rest of the body due to resistances against the presence of space. It can also cause disturbances in body balance, for it will affect the inner ear if any physical contractions are present in the ocular segment of the body armor.

Mark is a young professional man in his thirties, present in a Work group setting. Several women have been discussing the experience of a hole in their genital region. He tells me with some apprehension that he is afraid that he too has a hole in the genital area. From private sessions that I have done with him, I know that he has intense castration anxiety. I explore his experience of a hole in the lower part of his body by asking questions. Instantly, he starts becoming aware of a column of space inside his head. Here he experiences his mind as empty, clear, and with no thoughts. He feels, without any anxiety, that he has no physical boundaries around his cranium. He not only has a hole, the entire cranium is missing in his awareness.

This is a common action of space. It erases even the sense of body boundaries. Perhaps this phenomenon is the origin of the saying that a Zen master is a "man with no head." The loss of physical boundaries is experienced as a lack of separation between inside and outside. It is also felt as pleasant, freeing and unburdening.

Gradually, Mark becomes aware of all of himself as empty, pure nothingness, a void, a space. The column of space expands until his whole sense of himself is a lightness, an emptiness, a spaciousness. Mark mentions that he has no emotions. He experiences himself as a witness, a passive and silent witness. There is only space, and the space is aware, or the space is the awareness itself.

Here we see another dimension of space—the openness is also in the dimension of awareness. In fact, it is aware space. It is as though there is pure and open awareness at each point of the emptiness. This is what gives the sense of mental clarity, lucidity, and precision in such an experience.

In Mark's experience, space continued to expand until he felt himself as having no physical boundaries, with the space extending to infinity. Here then is the direct perception that the nature of the mind is really boundless space, literally boundless.

Besides directly sensing, intuiting, and being space, he could also see it. He could see it as emptiness, just like empty, physical space, but clear and immaculate. This is one of the common ways of seeing the inner space—as a clear and empty nothingness, the way we would imagine totally empty physical space. With eyes open, the physical environment is seen as it is, but with the more subtle perception of space pervading everything and extending infinitely.

It should be noted here that the experience of the column of space and of the mind as boundless space is usually the crown of the process of development of what some systems call the Kundalini. In this process, energy ascends up the spine into the head, causing all kinds of unusual experiences. However, when the process is successful, it culminates in the experience of boundless space. This experience is sometimes called the void, or "akash," a Sanskrit term. We will see later that this realization is not really the apex of human development. The void is the emptiness which in time will allow the unfolding of the fullness and richness of Being. Just as the void is the culmination point of the process of the ascent of energy, it will become the beginning point of a process of descent that will bring the fullness of Being.

To continue with Mark's experience, it seems that his sense of a hole in his genital region was actually the experience of the lower part of the column of space. At first he was aware only of the hole in the genital region because his attention was drawn to that area due to the focus of discussion in the group.

The experience of the lower part of the column of space is also connected to the experience of a hole in the "castrated" person. More accurately, the perception of the lack of the penis and the presence of a physical cavity develops into the experience of empty space only if the individual does not resist perception of the cavity and the affects accompanying it. However, most people report the emptiness as a darkness, as a dark and empty hole, which engenders fear in them. If the individual does not resist the perception of the dark and empty cavity, it will expand upward to include the entire pelvic area, the belly, and the rest of the body. So the perception of space will extend upward in this case.

Jane is a woman in her late twenties who has been involved in an intense love relationship with a young man. She is reporting her dissatisfaction in their contact and an unfulfilled longing for greater closeness and intimacy. She is crying, experiencing her dependent need for the man's presence. She starts experiencing a dark, empty cavity in the region of the genitals as she feels her dependent need and intense longing. I encourage her to allow the experience without identification. Here she starts experiencing a contraction in her throat and an impulse to swallow. We have already, in previous sessions, established the equivalence in her unconscious between her throat and her vagina. By bringing this to her attention she realizes that the feeling in the genital cavity is a desire to take in the man, to suck him in. As she experiences this, the cavity expands and the dark emptiness fills the whole belly, then the whole body. She feels she is a big, dark hole that desires to suck and take in the man. I see that her body has opened up in the middle revealing a dark emptiness. I feel she wants to enfold me into this emptiness.

In this example, we understand the deeper psychodynamic meaning of the genital cavity for the dependent woman. The sucking and swallowing tendency reveals the symbiotic wish at the root of the hungry emptiness. It is known in psychoanalysis that the desire for symbiotic merging can manifest as a desire for sucking in the man, a displacement of the oral wish for incorporation of the mother or her breast. In discussing the child's earliest fantasies, Jacobson says:

> Whenever he is fed by his mother or is physically close to her body, his wishful fantasies of complete reunion with the mother by means of (oral and visual, respiratory, skin) incorporation will be gratified. Hence, with the achievement of gratification, his images of the self and of the love object will temporarily merge, only to be severed again with the increase of instinctual needs and experiences of hunger, frustration, and real separation, which are apt to arouse aggression and libidinal desires. (Edith Jacobson, *The Self and the Object World*, p. 40.)

In our case history, Jane didn't want to go further to the perception of the symbiotic wish because of the presence of unconscious fears and rage toward her mother. But we can give additional case histories to illustrate how the genital cavity and the dark space are related to the symbiotic wish for merging.

First, we should note that the qualities of space as perceived in these cases vary: space is seen, for example, as clear or dark emptiness. The clear emptiness sometimes looks shiny. The space becomes a shining or glimmering void. More accurately described, it attains or becomes translucent, as if seen through cellophane. This happens either as a result of greater perceptual sensitivity or as a result of a deepening of the presence of space. Even the dark space can shine sometimes. It becomes a luminous blackness, as if the blackness has brilliancy. This feeling is similar to the experience of the peaceful and spacious darkness of the night. There is space and absolute stillness.

Returning to our discussion of the relation between the desire for merging and the experience of space, we examine additional case history material.

Penny is a beautiful young woman with a dependent self-image who has been experiencing difficulty in having the close intimate relationship she has longed for over many years. She has already become aware of the body-image of a cavity in the pelvic region, but has not yet admitted to wanting her mother. Every time she comes close to this feeling, she starts feeling frustrated and cold, which leads to feelings of anger toward her mother and to wishes of pushing her away. In this session, she starts by reporting how she is frustrated with her mother who has always given her conflicting messages—of not caring whether or not Penny spent time with her, but at the same time making her feel guilty if she did not do so. This content regresses her to childhood and to the feeling of frustration around the mother. She starts shivering and feeling cold and lonely. She feels that there is a huge emptiness inside and outside, dark and cold. She feels as if she is sitting on an iceberg. As she experiences this she realizes the absence of symbiotic gratification with her mother. She feels the dark, cold and lonely emptiness when she is alone, or when she remembers having had some close contact with her mother. Even when her mother held her as a child she felt cold and empty because her mother was cold and distant, and didn't want contact. So even in physical closeness she experienced the lack of symbiotic gratification which is why she had resisted the symbiotic wish, unconsciously knowing it would not be fulfilled.

What is important for us here is that while she is experiencing the lack of symbiotic gratification, she is experiencing space as a dark cold emptiness. In fact, the lack of symbiotic gratification is experienced by Penny as a dark and ice-cold emptiness, an unpleasant space. This unpleasant coldness, associated with empty space due to lack of symbiotic gratification, obviously adds to the self-image of deficiency, neediness, and dependency. So we see that the symbiotic wish lies at the bottom of the dependency needs. Gratification of the infantile dependency would

61

have fulfilled the symbiotic wish such that it would not have persisted unfulfilled into adulthood. The experience of the dark genital cavity or space as cold is common in people who have experienced the lack of phase appropriate symbiotic gratification. The coldness is, in fact, a somatic representation of the unfulfilled wish. However, there is another more fundamental reason why this coldness is associated with space. Unencumbered space is usually experienced as cool and fresh. It is frequently experienced as though one is lacking boundaries, and as the sensation of a cool breeze passing through. When the experience of space deepens, there is sometimes the sense that space is like clear ice. Some people feel as though they are at the North Pole. This reminds us of Penny's remark that she felt as if she were sitting on an iceberg. We will say more about this aspect later; now we will continue our exploration of the relation between space and the desire for merging.

We go back to the woman in our first example, Sandra. In another session, discussing her feelings of dependent longing for her distant husband, she starts experiencing the dark, empty cavity in the genital region. The hole expands into a dark tunnel or corridor. She is obviously describing here the column of space. She is afraid of this dark tunnel, afraid she will be swallowed up in it, fall into it—as if falling into an abyss. Obviously, this is object anxiety, but it is not yet clear since it is related to a desire for symbiotic merging. I encourage her to fall into the abyss. When she allows this, she experiences herself at the bottom of the tunnel, with the tunnel extending forward, away from her. She then feels she is the tunnel. When she identifies herself with the darkness and emptiness, she starts feeling the desire for swallowing the man, for taking him in. This acknowledgement for her symbiotic wish, first for her husband, then for me in the transference, transforms the dark tunnel. Because I do not reject her or her wish for symbiotic merging, the inner experience of the empty, dark tunnel changes into an experience of fullness. She sees the darkness becoming lighter and brighter. The transformation continues until the bright emptiness becomes a golden fullness. She feels full of a golden presence, pleasurable and fulfilling. She feels her boundaries disappearing, this time by melting into the environment rather than by being erased by space.

The method used here was Reichian breathing and direct work on the body armor. First the pelvic segment was relaxed, allowing for the experience of the hole. Loosening her diaphragmatic block, which in this case is the same as working through the fear of merging, transformed the darkness into golden fullness.

The golden fullness, which is often experienced as liquid honey with the sun shining through it, is the merged state itself, the longing for symbiotic fulfillment satisfied. Sandra feels soft, melted, merged with her surroundings. The experience is quite pleasurable, enjoyable and gratifying. She feels happy and contented. It is interesting to note here that I had never used the words "boundary" or "merged" in her presence, and that it is the first time that she herself used the word "merged."

Sandra is no longer experiencing empty space; it is as if the radiant golden fullness has filled the emptiness when the defenses against the wish for symbiotic merging have been dissolved. This is a rare state for most people, for everyone defends against real merging in avoidance of object anxiety.

It is interesting to note here that the desire for merging is not really a desire for another person, it is rather a desire for the merged state, the golden and sweet fullness. Because in the undeveloped infantile condition it was experienced with the mothering person, it becomes associated with being with, or merging with, another person. However, this golden fullness can be experienced alone, without the presence of another person. We will leave substantiation of this assertion for another publication, since it is not central to our investigation here. It is enough to state that many students who work through the fear of merging experience it frequently alone in moments of quietness. Sandra is really experiencing herself here as merging with her environment and not particularly with me. This point is of utmost importance in understanding intimate love relationships, because we know the desire for merging is at the core of the need for such relationships.

It is not uncommon for the merged state to arise when space is allowed. The other woman, Jane, in a later session, after working through her hatred toward her mother, enters the gold state of merging. In a Reichian breathing session, she starts telling me about a certain fear she has been having. She is separating from her boyfriend and is feeling a lot of sadness. She is feeling wounded and disappointed. Working on contractions in the pelvic segment and solar plexus, she starts crying, feeling the hurt. But she is also remembering what she feels when she is alone, for she doesn't understand the feeling. She reports feeling afraid of dying and disappearing. When I interpreted this as fear of the wish to disappear into somebody's arms, she starts experiencing the symbiotic wish. And slowly, she starts feeling very loving towards me. This state of love turns out to be the shiny golden state. The more she recognizes the state, the more it expands. She feels as if there are running rivers inside her. She feels pleasure, love, merging. She recognizes her feeling as what she has always sought in intimate relationships.

Frequently we find that behind the self-image of an empty cavity in a dependent person, there is a symbiotic wish, and that when resistances are worked through, the person experiences a golden fullness that is sometimes described as a golden womb, again denoting its symbiotic association. The next case illustrates all these steps happening in one session.

Nancy is a very attractive woman who is married, and also engaged in an intimate love relationship with another woman. In a Work group setting, we are discussing her sexual relationship with her woman friend. By interpreting her aggressive and masculine role in the relationship, she becomes aware of her unconscious belief that she possesses an invisible penis. She actually feels as if there is something physical protruding from her pubic area. By seeing this unconscious body-image, she feels the penis changing, as if it has inverted inward. Then she feels a dark elongated cavity inside her pelvic area. This gets her in touch with her dependent needs. I ask her what it is she wants from the woman who is her lover. Here she becomes aware of her symbiotic wish.

She talks about feeling warm, cozy, safe and secure in the arms of this woman. She describes the feeling as being a warm golden womb. She feels a satisfying fullness in her belly.

Space is not always needed for experiencing the merged state, nor does space always lead to this golden merged state. But allowing the experience of the symbiotic wish without resistance or fear always leads to the golden merged fullness. And as we have seen, awareness of the empty cavity, whose connection with space we will further elucidate in later chapters, often brings awareness of the symbiotic wish.

Martin is a professional married man, in this session confronting some marital difficulties. He talks about the possibility of separating from his wife. Here he gets a bronchial reaction, a difficulty in breathing. He feels fear of suffocation. He then remembers feeling this way as a baby; this makes him feel yearning for his mother. But he then experiences a rigidity in his body, as if there is a solid film spreading all over his body. By staying quiet for a while and breathing gently, he feels the solid film slowly melting. It becomes fluid, alive, and golden. He experiences an intense happiness, a pleasurable melting.

Our main interest here, however, is not in the golden merged state but in space and its connection to merging. The fact that, in some cases, the emptiness of space leads into a fulfilling golden fullness gives us a glimpse of the further uses of space, of the creative aspect of space. The golden fullness is not the only fruit of the creativity of space. We have discussed it briefly only as an example to illustrate the creative dimension of space. The creativity of space is boundless. In fact, the experience of space itself can develop and deepen into a higher form of space, a space that is neither empty nor full. It is a dimension of space where the physical boundaries of the body are not erased by emptiness, but experienced as space itself. In this case, space simultaneously holds two opposites: emptiness and fullness. It feels empty and light, but also feels full and has density. Space here is not an absence, but a presence. This is unfamiliar for the ordinary mind. However, this unfamiliarity is only a boundary that can be dissolved, or in this case itself seen as a space. This phenomenon is known in Buddhism and referred to as the unity of emptiness and form. The *prajna-paramita sutra* says: "Form is empty, emptiness is form; form is no other than emptiness, emptiness is no other than form." (Chogyam Trungpa, *op. cit.*, p. 188.)

Some of the characteristics of this full space can be seen in the following letter written by a student who had experienced space in her private session with me:

> As I started breathing into my chest and exhaling into my belly, I became aware of being angry. My anger had been toward certain people for still not seeing that I care for them very much, and feeling that they had been rejecting my friendliness and caring.
>
> When you had me go back to the breathing, I became aware of an emptiness filled with a fullness. You touched my forehead and eyes and it intensified. I felt groggy, and the fullness felt thick and cool, yet empty. I could feel that space at the top of my head, which felt open and cool.
>
> I felt the fullness get lighter and vary in density. I felt that I was expanding and I felt this presence move throughout my body. I actually could feel my uterus and felt I could see it. I felt my genitals and my vagina as being soft like my uterus. I felt I was experiencing no boundaries to my body. I felt wonderful, as if I had no cares in the world. I felt like I wanted to play and laugh, like I could fly away.

This form of space sometimes feels cold like ice, but the feeling is pleasant and fresh. There is a sense that one is on the North Pole when the crisp expansion of space merges with coldness of ice. However, when there are resistances in the body or unconscious distortions in body-image, the sensation can be of heat and burning. It feels as if there is a fire burning away the resistances, the blockages, the impurities. In another session, Pamela is talking to me privately and is already feeling space. She feels as if there is a balloon in her belly. She is aware of tension in her shoulders.

She starts feeling the space going up her body, empty and full at the same time, like an inflated balloon full of space, but she feels only pockets of it in her back and chest due to some physical tensions. She starts feeling a burning sensation spreading across her back and shoulders. I realize there is some resistance there and ask her how she feels about her arms and shoulders. With tears and embarrassment she says she feels her shoulders are too small and narrow, and her arms too thin. This surprises me, because she does not look this way; but then I remember that about four years ago, she was much thinner. I see that although her body changed, her body-image has not; so I ask her to look at her shoulders and arms in the mirror. When she does, she starts crying and tells me that they don't look the way they look in her mind. She starts remembering how her parents teased her about her small shoulders and thin arms. This brought up sadness and anger at them. But most importantly, the burning intensified, then stopped, leaving only space in the upper belly and a body-image that was new for her. As she put it:

> I feel huge when there is space in my upper body, and unfamiliar with myself. . . . What you said about believing my old image of myself explains a lot. I expected to see my old caved-in posture. I felt surprised not to see it, surprised and glad.

In this chapter, then, we have seen that the action of space as allowed to manifest in the process of investigating unconscious self-images and the affects associated with them, not only corrects the distortions in self-image, but can deepen into a profound understanding of the nature of mind, and further, allow new realms of experience to emerge. Here, in this greater space, we are not only dealing with the nature of the mind. Our exploration is taking us from the mind into the realm of Being, what we will call essence.

PART TWO

The Void
and
Transformation

CHAPTER THIRTEEN

Space and Essence

Exploration of the self-image and its relation to space can stand as a separate and self-sufficient approach to self-understanding, so profound are the results of this method. The techniques admit of great refinement and extension leading to increasingly subtle levels. Here, however, we will briefly discuss the discovery and development of essence, or Being, to show how this aspect of reality arises in the context of work on self-image, and further to demonstrate the tremendous usefulness of space in relation to essential development. (A more thorough discussion of essential development appears in our book, *Essence* (Samuel Weiser, 1986).)

Spiritual and metaphysical schools have always maintained that there is more to a human being than the usual personality whose categories of experience are limited to physical sensations, emotions, and mental thoughts and images. For this reason, many adherents of these schools criticize and even reject Western psychology and psychoanalysis; for the various formulations of psychology do not admit of other categories of experience. Similarly, then, psychologists of most persuasions either ignore or reject the ideas of the spiritual and metaphysical schools.

The aspect of a human being that is not the product of physical heredity, environment or upbringing, is sometimes referred to as Essence or Being. The great Sufi philosopher Ibn 'Arabi's notion of this subtle level of reality has been described thus:

> The Name latif or "Subtle" with this particular connotation represents the Absolute as a Substance (jawhar) which, immaterial and invisible, permeates and pervades the entire world of Being just as a color permeates substances. This Substance which is infinitely variable runs through everything and constitutes its reality. (Toshihiko Izutsu, *Sufism and Taoism*, p. 141.)

The Sufis hold that Essence is one, but manifests in different qualities or aspects; and as we have seen, these qualities, which are part of the deep nature of a human being, can be readily experienced when the personality identifications which block the experience of space are surrendered and space is allowed.

G.I. Gurdjieff, a Russian teacher of essential development, gives a clear differentiation between personality and essence:

> It must be understood that man consists of two parts: *essence* and *personality*. Essence in man is what is *his own*, personality in man is what is "not his own." "Not his own" means what has come from outside, what he has learned, or reflects, all traces of exterior impressions left in the memory and in the sensations, all words and movements that have been learned, all feelings created by imitation—all this is "not his own," all this is personality. . . .
>
> A small child has no personality yet. He is what he really is. He is essence. His desires, tastes, likes, dislikes, express his being such as it is. . . .
>
> Essence is the truth in man; personality is the false. But in proportion as personality grows, essence manifests itself more and more rarely, and more and more

feebly, and it very often happens that essence stops in its growth at a very early age and grows no further. It happens very often that the essence of a grown up man, even that of a very intellectual and, in the accepted meaning of the word, highly "educated" man, stops on the level of a child of five or six. (P.D. Ouspensky, *In Search of the Miraculous*, pp. 162-163.)

Buddhist sources refer to this fundamental essence as "Dharma-kaya," "Buddha nature," "Bodhicitta," and other terms denoting different qualities of essential reality. Herbert Guenther, quoting a Tibetan Buddhist treatise, says:

> All sentient beings possess the nature of Buddha-hood, continuously present since its beginningless beginning. What is this nature of Buddhahood? It is the existential fact and presence of mind; since it is intrinsically pure [it is] the beginningless time-encompassing dimension of Being (Dharmadatu) unbroken, impartial, radiant in itself, as the pristine existential experience of Being (Dharmakaya). (Herbert Guenther, *The Tantric View of Life*, p. 124.)

Another Buddhist source, Trungpa Rinpoche, makes clear the relation between the experience of space (shunyata) and the experience of Being:

> The shunyata experience corresponds to the level of a bodhisattva. But the shunyata experience is in a sense incomplete from the point of view of the next stage, which is the experience of prabhasavra, luminosity. Prabhasavra is the ultimate positive experience. Sunyata is like the sky. That space of the sky being there, it becomes possible for cosmic functions to take place within it. It becomes possible for there to develop sunrise and sunset. In the same way, within the space of shunyata, of openness and freedom, it becomes possible for students to begin to deal with the actual experiences of non-duality. This is the prabhasavra experience, which is a way of acknowledging the Buddha-nature that exists within one. (Chogyam Trungpa, *The Dawn of Tantra*, p. 35.)

Although most psychologists limit the realm of their investigation to "ordinary" categories of experience, psychoanalysis and object relations theory do hypothesize the existence of inborn, unconditioned aspects of the individual. Freud's concepts of libido and drive might be seen as close to the concept of an essential nature, and Hartmann added the concept of inborn ego apparatuses.

> The individual does not acquire all the apparatuses which are put into the service of the ego in the course of development; perception, motility, intelligence, etc., rest on constitutional givens. (Heinz Hartmann, *Ego Psychology and the Problem of Adaptation*, p. 101.)

Some systems, particularly the various Buddhist schools and some Hindu systems, attempt the realization and development of essence by first cultivating the experience of space. So their meditation techniques are usually directed towards the perception of the nature of the mind as void or emptiness. The practice of Vipassana meditation of the Theravada school is directed, for instance, towards the cultivation of panoramic awareness, or what we have called "aware space." Zen Buddhist techniques direct the practitioner towards emptiness, the void, "shunyata." However, this is not taken to be the end of the Buddhist path, a point stressed by the Tibetan Vajrayana schools of Buddhism as reflected in the quote from Trungpa Rinpoche above.

From the experience of empty space, due to its aspect of creativity, the experience of essence or Being unfolds, as we have shown in the example of the golden merged state. The Buddhists tend to cultivate the universal (by universal we mean here not limited by separating boundaries, either physical or otherwise) aspects of Being first, culminating in the realization of what is called Dharmakaya or Buddha nature. Then the personal (by personal we mean here the contrasting opposite of impersonal) aspect of essence is developed, related to what is called Nirmanakaya or Being in-the-world. Space or emptiness is a requirement, a first step toward the unfolding of essence. The personal aspect of essence is left to the last stages, probably to avoid confusing the personal aspect with the usual sense of personal identity, the ego-identity.

The rigid frozenness and defensive separateness of the ego identity is first relaxed by the dissolution of the boundaries of the self-image, a process that culminates in the experience of space.

However, not all schools of essential development follow the same progression. And not all of them require space as a stepping stone towards the unfolding of essence. For instance, the Sufis sometimes develop the personal aspects of essence first. The personal essence is usually referred to as the "pearl beyond price." In many of their teaching stories the seeker is either attempting to free an imprisoned princess with the name of "incomparable pearl" or is looking for a rare and precious gem. Here is one form of this story, taken from some gnostic writings, with the title of "The Hymn of the Pearl":

> When I was a little child
> and dwelt in the kingdom of my
> Father's house,
> and took joy in the wealth
> and glory of my upbringing,
> my parents gave me provisions and sent
> me out from our homeland in the East.

> They take off his glorious robes and send him down to Egypt to fetch the pearl, which is guarded by a snake. On his arrival there, he puts on Egyptian clothes, and they drug him into forgetting his past and his mission. His father sends him a letter to awaken him. He charms the snake, seizes the pearl, takes off the filthy and impure clothes he is wearing. His parents send his robe to greet him.

> Suddenly, as I looked straight at it,
> the robe seemed like a mirror-image of
> myself,
> I saw myself entire in it,
> in looking at it I was looking at myself.

> So he returns, and does obeisance to his Father, who promises him that with his pearl he shall enter the presence of the King of Kings. (John Ferguson, *Encyclopaedia of Mysticism*, p. 82.)

The experience of space in all of its gradations is referred to by Sufis as "fana," meaning the dissolution of the usual sense of identity which happens at various points in the seeker's development. Then the universal aspects of essence are developed, aspects referred to in this story as the Father, the King of Kings, and the robe.

This is usually put in a religious language: "Whoso knoweth himself knoweth his lord," a saying attributed to Mohammed. So the experience of space, when self-boundaries are dissolved, is seen as a transitional stage and the beginning of the entry into the universal or boundless aspects.

Here, the experience of emptiness (fana) heralds the advent of the experience of essence without the presence of individual identity. This is a cataclysmic transformation in which experience itself, from being bounded by an individual center and limitations (sense of identity), is opened up. There is no more individual experience of essence or Being. There is only Being, boundless and infinite. This is what is usually referred to as cosmic consciousness or the divine Being.

The birth (finding) and development of the personal essence has to do with the issues of symbiosis and separation-individuation. This is because the personal essence is the real person, which is usually usurped by the ego-personality.

In our exploration, we have approached the work on essential development from the perspective of self-image and its relation to space. But we can select any aspect of essence, of which there are many, and show the psychodynamic means for its development. In the last chapter we discussed briefly the aspect of the merged golden state. Another aspect, for example, the aspect of absolute value, or essence as value, can best be understood in its relation to the development of self-esteem, from narcissism to superego valuation. Or we can consider the aspect of the personal essence and see its relation to the development of the ego and its sense of identity. Here we will focus on the process of identification and on the relationship between the development of ego and the development of personal essence.

The development of ego and sense of personal identity depends, as we have seen, on the process of identification, culminating in the formation of a self-image. We have seen that the formation of self-representations is a process of freezing boundaries in the emptiness of the mind. In contrast, the pearl beyond price, the personal aspect of essence, is a sense of personal identity that does not depend on self-representation, and hence, does not depend on the existence or the defending of boundaries in open space. In fact, its development comes about through the undoing of these identifications. The culmination of the elimination of identifications is the birth of the pearl beyond price, or the discovery of one's own essential person-hood, one's personal nature that does not depend on the past. This is an aspect of Being that is not understood or appreciated until it is experienced. When it manifests, one cannot but be filled with wonder at the majesty, beauty, and richness of essence.

Psychodynamic understanding has, then, an extraordinary power and potential far beyond its therapeutic uses. The existing body of knowledge in the field of psychology, and especially in psychoanalysis, can be very effectively used for essential development. And the nature of psychodynamic understanding allows us to work directly with the present experience of the student without following any particular progression or gradation. We can simply understand what is there in the moment, and this will lead us naturally to a particular aspect of essence: space, the personal aspect, the universal aspect, or any of several others.

Using understanding in this way, we can avoid the awkwardness and inefficiency of many traditional techniques, such as giving all students the same meditations, the same physical exercises, or the same advice on the value of surrender regardless of the specific situation or state of the student. Psychodynamic understanding deals exactly with whatever situation the student presents, with what is actually of vital interest to him and his life. And from this real situation, understanding will lead him to the particular aspect of essence that is actually relevant to him at the time.

As he continues the process of self-understanding, now with awareness of his own essence, the other aspects will appear and develop. This will happen naturally and spontaneously if the person looks at the truth in his experience. The essence is gradually freed from the grip of the unconscious and assumes its rightful place as the conscious center of one's life. (See our book, *The Elixir of Enlightenment*, Samuel Weiser, 1984, for a more detailed discussion of this point.)

CHAPTER FOURTEEN

Space and Sexuality

As most of our case histories have shown, and as we discussed in Chapter 11, space arises most readily when dealing with body-image. Sometimes a person comes to experience space by considering other kinds of self-representations, but for most people it is confronting the "genital hole" that causes space initially to arise. This, as we have seen, is the experience of the genital area as a dark, empty hole, with no anatomical parts. The individual feels, and sometimes envisions, a lack, an absence between the thighs. The experience can be very definite and clear, with the boundaries of the hole clearly demarcated. It almost feels like a physical experience, even though the individual is always aware that the hole is not physical. The definiteness and clarity of the perception of the genital hole never fails to astound the person; it is always unexpected.

Within the boundaries of the genital hole there is the sensation of nothingness, of voidness, of no existence. If the person senses or looks deeper, the nothingness deepens and expands. The hole expands into more of the pelvis and later into the rest of the body. Under normal circumstances, awareness of this hole in the unconscious body-image is defended against through many different means. The most obvious is physical contraction, tension. Typically there is a tension around the pelvis, centered at the sacrum and the perineum. This ring of tension is normally accompanied by another tension ring around the head, especially around the ocular region. We recall that the genital hole is one end of a column of emptiness running through the body, so we see then that there are tensions which block the two ends of this column or tube. There are other tension patterns in the body relating to the column, but the pelvis and head are the major and most frequently encountered ones.

Of course, these tension patterns and the psychodynamic defense mechanisms that go with them are generally unconscious. They surface to consciousness only when the individual is approaching awareness of the genital hole and the psychological material associated with it. The tension in the head manifests in extreme cases as headaches. The tension in the pelvis can lead to all kinds of sexual difficulties.

The importance of the genital hole becomes obvious when we realize that it is a universal phenomenon. We find that it is part of the unconscious self-image in all individuals, men and women, without exception. It does not signify pathology or neurosis. It is part of the normal self-image of every person, albeit unconscious. The only possible exceptions are those who do not defend against space. If a person can experience space completely and consciously, then there will be no genital hole in the self-image.

This assertion might sound preposterous to many, but it becomes understandable if we comprehend the relationship between space and the genital hole. We have discussed space as the true nature of the mind. As well, we have discussed essence or true being in its various aspects and manifestations. We have also seen that most people do not normally experience either essence or space. This means that the identity or self-image of the normal person does not include space.

Also, we have seen that the self-image itself is a kind of barrier against the experience of space; in fact, it is the barrier. It is what fills the space, what structuralizes it; so only an individual who can let go of identification with the self-image will be able to experience space. (There is actually a gradation here; the self-image manifests from a fairly superficial preconscious level to extremely deep and subtle ones; likewise, the experience of space can range from a simple openness and dissolution of the usual self-image to a sense of complete annihilation of the sense of self. These gradations will be discussed in Chapter 20.)

However, space is an integral part of the person. It is the true nature of his mind. This means that his self-image contains a big distortion; it excludes a large part of him—space itself. This distortion of self-image manifests as the genital hole.

Why is the unconscious self-image of the genital hole so crucial to the experience of space? There is no simple theoretical answer to this question; in fact, the idea at first seems unlikely and mysterious. Our first understanding of this relationship came from consistent, though surprising, experiential observations with many individuals. The genital hole is consistently the entry to the experience of space and emptiness.

Other than the well-known Freudian theory of the castration complex, which is more a description of how the mind relates to the experience of a blocking or deficiency in the genital area than a causal explanation of the hole, there may be several factors which contribute to the importance of the phenomenon of the genital hole in the self-image. Both the genital pleasure of orgasm and the symbiotic pleasure of nursing that releases the orgastic reflex in the infant involve a "melting" of the boundaries of experience, and often a sense of merging with another person. This may be experienced as somehow a direct threat to the sense of the individual's constructed self-image. The orgasm is often referred to as "le petit mort"—the little death. As we have seen many times, the dissolution of boundaries always involves the arising of space, and the functioning of sexuality involves a flow of being which tends to temporarily dissolve boundaries and would thus tend toward the experience of space. The causality could go any number of ways in this complex; for instance, blocking the flow of physical and subtle energies in the genitals could be motivated by the attachment to the sense of rigid self-boundaries, and so be seen as a defense against the dissolving effects of space which would arise if the flow were allowed.

Both Freud and Wilhelm Reich wrote a great deal about the cultural factors and childrearing practices which lead to blocks in sexuality. In our work it is clear, both experientially and theoretically, that the blocking of both space and essence in the genitals is a critical issue in our work on the dissolution of the various levels of self-image.

We must also remember that the genital hole is only the lower part of a column of emptiness that goes through the body, as we have discussed. This column of emptiness is really nothing but the presence of space, seen in the presence of finite boundaries constituting the concept of the person. This means that the genital hole is the presence of space that is still obscured by the unconscious attachment to self-boundaries. We will discuss this point more fully in Chapter 19.

Whatever the reason behind the observation that when space is lost the deficiency appears as the genital hole, it is a consistent fact and seems to be a universal one. It is the reason that the acceptance and understanding of the genital hole readily leads to the experience of clear space, and it also explains our assertion that the genital hole is a universal unconscious part of the self-image, because space is universally not experienced.

Babs is a married woman in her early thirties, very conscious of her physical image, and concerned with what people think of her. She has been having a recurrent frightening dream for a few months. Understanding the dream leads her to feeling a sense of emptiness in her pelvis. This frightens her, and she resists the experience. She writes to me later:

> I feel that what you have said is true. I am afraid to feel the emptiness. When I do allow myself to feel it (emptiness) I feel less anxious, and more myself. I am

not too sure these days who "myself" is. When I stop fighting it and just allow myself to feel it, I feel more peaceful and calm, as you say, more of who I really am.

I can't help but wonder, if all this time I am not the image who I thought I was, then who am I?

As we see, Babs' sense of identity starts to change when she experiences space. She maintains some distance from her self-image. It's interesting to note here that her self-image at first included an invisible penis. The unconscious belief that she possessed a penis gave her a certain phallic identification which was reflected in her conscious body image. It also put her at odds with men—competing with them, attempting to "castrate" them. This belief in the invisible penis, which constituted a major part of her self-image, turned out to be a defense against the genital hole. So losing her "penis" meant more than that; it meant losing her phallic image and all the aspects of her psychic structure which had depended on this image.

In our earlier case histories we discussed how the genital hole is precipitated by allowing feelings of inadequacy, inferiority, passivity, dependency, weakness; it did not reflect a sexual image exclusively. This is both true and untrue.

It is true in that the genital hole signifies not only the absence of space in the normal person's realm of experience, but it also signifies the absence of essence in its various aspects. As we saw in the section on essential development, space is needed as a ground for the experience of essence. Even when essence is experienced before space is integrated, it does not become a permanent experience. It can become a permanent part of our experience only after space is integrated. This phenomenon is understood by most spiritual teachings.

So the absence of space also signifies absence or lack of essence in its various aspects—such as strength, will, value, personal essence, and so on. The genital hole is frequently experienced as associated with these lacks.

On the other hand, the statement that the genital hole does not reflect a basically sexual self-image can be seen as untrue.

It does reflect the image of having no genitals. In fact, it is common for women who feel these lacks to attribute them to the lack of a penis. Babs felt exactly these lacks when she lost her imaginary "penis." However, in her case, the usual identification is with the phallus; other women, passive or dependent types, identify with the hole itself.

This phenomenon can be illustrated in the case history of a man with a passive dependent identification and his experience of a genital hole.

Bart is a young man in his late twenties, of quiet demeanor and unobtrusive personality. He always has difficulties with his aggressive girlfriend, because he can't assert himself with her. After talking to me a few times, he writes:

> Several weekends ago, I wanted to come and talk with you privately. However, I wasn't clear about what it was I wanted to talk with you about. As we spoke, I became aware of feeling weak and void of power, and finally realized I was feeling emasculated. The feeling of emasculation felt bad and shameful, especially speaking to you. I wanted to hide and not let you know about it (or any other man). I felt in my body that my penis and groin area were gone, and that I had nothing but empty space there. I realized that my mother had emasculated and castrated me, as did my father. The feeling of emptiness triggered in me deep sadness. However, the sadness left and dissipated, and I felt rage and anger towards my mother, in its place.

He then relates how the emptiness led to the activation of his will—a sense of purpose, determination and strength.

The approach of space is experienced as a sense of lack as it pushes the genital hole to consciousness. The genital hole is always reacted to as a castration. If the castration is related to physically, then the individual sees it as the absence of the penis; this is so for both men and women. If it is related to psychologically, then it is seen as the lack of will, strength, value, and so on. It is no wonder that many people associate these lacks with the absence of a penis. Even when space is experienced without going through the genital hole, we find that the main barrier is at the genitals. We see this clearly in the account of Jackson, a man in his late thirties, who has been working with me for about two years.

> My feelings had been heightened the day before in the private session, when I felt abandoned by you, the first time I had been aware of this. I felt like you didn't hear what I was saying, your attention was not in the room and to top it all, you didn't want to have dinner with me.
>
> In the group session, I still felt angry and there was a clarity about it; I didn't feel like "poor me." I just wanted your attention, damn it! I could feel it in my bones and I was going to make the demand regardless.
>
> You asked me to sense my chest. Right in the center, it felt empty; clear and empty. "Feel it," you said, "and let it expand." This began a process that seemed to last a long time (on the other hand, I was not conscious of the time). I felt very safe and cared for—strange. The emptiness began to expand, and slowly it began to be more like a sense of space than just of emptiness. I felt good, soft, melting, as though my body was fading away.
>
> You asked me if the whole body was gone. I realized that only my penis was left. Seeing this, the image of the penis dissolved.
>
> I could not look at you; my eyes were fixed on the floor. Your voice had an unreal quality about it, and yet I could hear every word. I felt like you were guiding me and I felt safe, even though my body parts seemed lighter, less visible, and less significant. I had no doubt that I was still present, even though my body was not as much there, and I seemed to be present in a different way—more present (in intensity). I remember thinking that I ought to be afraid and I wasn't.

We see here that Jackson started with a lack, a lack of value and compassion. He experienced this deficiency in the chest. This led to space. But space stopped acting when it got to the genitals. Jackson didn't want to let go of his penis. This resistance, the fear of losing the cherished penis, always manifests in those with masculine identification, both men and women.

Let us now try to make some order out of these findings relating space and sexual image:

The structuralization of self-image, as well as other childhood experience, leads to the loss of space as part of our experience. Along with space, and due to other factors, essence in its various aspects is lost. Self-image ends up excluding emptiness and the fullness of essence as possible categories of experience.

These losses are related to all kinds of lacks and deficiencies. The loss of space affects the self-image by creating an unconscious body-image with a genital hole. In fact, the genital hole is simply, as we have mentioned, the lower part of an empty tube. Sometimes the hole is felt at the top of the head. So space and essence are replaced by a personality, based on a constructed self-image, whose core is a deficient emptiness which is experienced as an empty tube at the core of the body. This emptiness is felt as the lack of such qualities as love, value, joy, strength, will, autonomy or sense of self. It manifests in the self-image as weakness, dependency, castration, worthlessness, inferiority, and so on. As we said earlier, this genital hole with its accompanying emotional associations is a universal phenomenon. Everybody develops a self-image. However, individuals differ in the way they relate to this hole depending on their personal history. The relationship to this lack determines to a great degree the character of the individual and his overall self-image and sense of identity.

The deficiency associated with the genital hole develops very early in childhood in the process of ego development, that is, in the first two years of life. So the child acquires an unconscious sense of having an empty hole at the genital region. This has far-reaching consequences for character formation.

For instance, we believe it is this unconscious experience of having no genitals which leads to the preoccupation with castration at the genital and oedipal stages of psychosexual development. Freud believed that the fear of castration, or the belief in it, occurs when the child discovers the sexual differences between boys and girls. Girls start feeling castrated, and boys become afraid of losing their penis.

We believe that the discovery of sexual difference contributes, among other things, to the castration complex. However, Freud had no idea that children had an actual sense of a hole in the genital area. It is difficult to directly prove this, but we believe that the presence of the genital hole in the unconscious self-image is the primary factor behind the castration complex. Unconsciously, the child feels he has nothing there. In a boy, this unconscious feeling will probably make him feel insecure about his penis. In a girl, the hole with its associated lacks gets connected to the vagina, an association that can easily lead to the belief that her lacks are due to the absence of a penis.

We have seen in many of our case histories that the hole is connected in the mind to the absence of a penis, both for males and females. The initial associations and judgments which arise when it is encountered are also connected to the absence of a penis. For these reasons, it would not be surprising to discover that the unconscious presence of the genital hole (and its association to the absence of a penis) is one of the main factors underlying the old chauvinistic myth that strength, will, and intelligence are masculine qualities. This is because the genital hole is connected emotionally to the lack of will, strength, intelligence and other qualities, on the one hand, and to the absence of a penis on the other.

Some men and women identify so strongly with the genital hole that it becomes a central part of their self-image. These are the passive feminine characters, who experience themselves as weak, dependent, worthless, and so on. These people often feel that they are stupid, brainless. This last is understandable; the genital hole is accepted, although not completely consciously, so the defense against it is not complete. This allows it to sometimes expand into the column of space which, when it reaches the head, tends to silence the thoughts. The absence of thoughts and the slowness in the linear thinking process that results is then judged as lack of mental intelligence. However, this calm and empty mental state, although it is judged as stupidity, is really a peaceful and beautiful state. It is the beginning of the experience of space with its mental peace and relaxation.

The passive feminine woman usually believes that she accepts her vagina, that she accepts being a woman. This is also a cultural myth. These women are not actually complete women; they are somewhat feminine only because they do not believe unconsciously that they have a penis. However, they do not accept the reality of the vagina, or if they do, they usually do not value it. Such women value the man for his penis, and devalue themselves, and so are usually subservient to the man. Their identification is not with the vagina, but with the empty hole.

The same pattern happens in the passive feminine man, who feels and behaves as if he is castrated. Although he sees that he has a penis, his sexual sense of self comes from the identification with the empty genital hole. Many such men have sexual identifications with mother, i.e., they believe unconsciously that they have a vagina. The unconscious self-image of having an invisible vagina develops in certain sets of circumstances in the formative years which lead to a very strong sexual mother identification.

David is a professional man in his mid-thirties. He has been involved in the work of self-understanding for several years. He has understood many things about himself, but there is a curious character trait that seems not to change at all. He always responds to situations in an emotional way which reminds him of his mother. This would not have been curious (since every individual has mother identification) but for the fact that he seemed always to defend himself against feelings of castration. His frequent emotional response was to be tearful and passive. At one of his private sessions I suggested, when he was having this habitual response, that he sense the area of his pelvis. He could sense a certain softness at his perineum. Staying with this softness, he felt it developing. He began feeling very soft and juicy in the area, along with a sense of light "fluffiness." It was a big surprise for him, difficult to believe, but he was determined to understand this part of himself, because it caused him so much trouble, especially in the sphere of intimate relations. The softness in the perineum expanded and started to feel like a soft and juicy vagina. He described actually seeing an image of a soft, pink vagina in that area. This made sense to him because it went along with the character trait he was concerned with. It was the self-representation responsible for his curious emotional responses. Here, he started seeing some new aspects of his relationship with his mother—for instance, that by having the unconscious image of the soft and juicy vagina, he felt that he had his mother's softness and love. This initiated an intense and sometimes painful process of self-understanding. Of course, seeing the image of the vagina brought about the experience of space. He was enfolded in a black space, which indicated a shift in the inner self-image and the sense of identity.

It is not uncommon that men with exaggerated external phallic identification are covering up an unconscious identification with the vagina. The exaggerated penis is supposed to hide and to distract from the softness and juiciness that is judged by the man's superego as weak and effeminate.

However, under most circumstances, men with exaggerated masculinity, who are trying to exhibit a big and powerful phallus, who put up a facade of toughness, strength, and iron will—in other words, those with the "macho" image—are men who are trying to defend against the genital hole by exaggerating and holding on tightly to the phallic identification. The greater the fear of castration, the greater is the need to defend and exaggerate the phallic image. This is well known in depth psychology. What we are adding here is the connection of the fear of castration to the fear of the genital hole. Whether a man unconsciously identifies with the genital hole or with the phallic defense depends primarily on the circumstances of his early childhood. Those so-called "masculine" men usually have a difficult time experiencing and accepting the genital hole. It brings a lot of fear and humiliation, actually a cataclysmic breakdown in the defensive structure of the personality.

The phallic man's fear of the genital hole is exceeded only by the phallic woman's fear of losing her imaginary penis. The man is afraid because of his unconscious genital hole and because of the childhood oedipal situation. The woman's fear, on the other hand, is greater, because the threat to her "penis" is greater. Not only does she have an unconscious genital hole, her imagined penis is always threatened by reality. Every time the woman sees her genitals, she can see she has no real penis. So reality itself becomes a great threat; it is always pointing to the genital hole. This insecurity manifests as exaggerated and unrealistic competition with men, and all kinds of attempts, conscious and unconscious, to cut them down to size, that is, to castrate them. Such phallic women usually despise and reject the passive feminine woman because she is a reminder of their greatest fear.

These women hold on to their phallic identifications for dear life. Space is fought and defended against. The following letter from Donna, who has been struggling with this issue for some time, reveals some of these defenses:

> Thinking about writing you my experience of working with you makes me aware that I usually think about my experience rather than just experience it. My experience is usually fleeting because of interruptions by my thoughts.

> I experienced feeling female, but it was brief. However, I trust now that I do sometimes know how a girl feels. I do not trust my experiencing of feeling space. I usually doubt that I ever really did and now I doubt I really did in the group night.

> Several times while we talked, I felt barriers come up. I am not aware of why or when but it happens to me often and I feel nothing. Or I feel distant from being able to feel or sense.

> I also experienced wanting to hide or get away a lot. When I am working with you I do not notice feeling uncomfortable in the group, until I feel threatened. I usually feel threatened when I feel emptiness in my pelvis. Then I automatically tighten my legs. I am then real aware of the group and want to hide.

We see that one of her defenses is thinking instead of experiencing. Thinking fills the mind, and in this way defends against the emptiness of space. Thinking is in fact the inner experience that corresponds to the ring of tension around the head. Doubt is an especially efficient form of this defense, because doubt involves a tightening of the forehead and the eyes, and the centers of perception in the ocular region. This not only prevents the experience of space, it also invalidates past experiences of it. The fact is that Donna has experienced space many times before. She has graphically seen her fantasized penis, has identified the tensions in her pelvis that correspond to it, and has experienced the genital hole many times. Yet she is still afraid. Accepting space means a change of identity, and that is why she does not trust it. In fact, she considers space an enemy that is going to take away her defenses. She likes feeling like a female when she accepts space and feels her real genitals, but then she gets frightened. For her, accepting space and her real genitals means a totally different way of being and living. It means she has to be real, something new to her.

It's interesting to note that her issue presented itself at one point as a feeling of hardness and difficulty in feeling softness, but at another point as concern with her thinking. She thought furiously, and didn't want to stop thinking. Thinking and having a penis were inseparable for her. We believe that this association between linear thinking and having a penis might be the main reason for the cultural myth that men are better than women at logical thinking, and that women are more intuitive. This myth might be primarily due to the blockage against space and the various relationships people have with the resulting genital hole. Intuition comes when the mind is empty; it is connected with space. Linear thinking in its compulsive mode is a result of blockage of space in the head.

After space is experienced and integrated, we find a gradual integration of both logical and intuitive capacities in the same individual, male or female. An integrated person has both capacities. The essence, our true being, is neither male nor female. The sexual differences are primarily physical and physiological.

From this developmental picture there arise many insights. First, we see that the fear of castration in both men and women is profoundly a fear of the genital hole. Of course, it may also be due to more specific circumstances in childhood which add to and justify the fear.

This understanding explains why in psychotherapy, and even in psychoanalysis, the experience of space is not usually encountered. During therapy, especially deep therapy, the individual at some point reaches the Oedipus complex and the castration complex connected to it. The analyst or therapist understands the castration fear only as due to fear of the oedipal rival and to the knowledge of sexual differences. So the emphasis is on dealing with the fear and seeing how it is unrealistic. Thus the person in therapy rarely goes beyond the fear of castration.

The therapist is not aware that the state of castration is actually there as the genital hole. Even if the state of castration surfaces, the therapist would usually not allow himself to see it as more than an emotional state of castration. To actually experience the absence of the genitals is not envisioned as possible. This mindset in the therapist, then, actually reinforces the defenses of the client who does not wish to experience the state of castration— the genital hole.

This means that the fear of castration in the phallic types and the castration identification of the passive feminine types might never be resolved completely in therapy. As long as the empty genital hole exists in the unconscious self-image and is defended against, there is no fundamental change in these character types. Analysis or therapy only brings about an amelioration of symptoms by understanding and resolving the childhood conflicts which contributed to the castration issue: such developments as the oedipal situation and the various identifications with both parents. The self-image basically continues, unchanged and unchallenged. The identification with the self-image and the personality is not broken. Space is not allowed, and thus neither is the essence allowed.

We see then that present-day depth psychology cannot lead to fundamental transformation. Fundamental transformation happens only with the breakthrough to space and to the realm of essence. This is why we believe that our study in this book can be of fundamental significance to depth psychology. Depth psychology can become a comprehensive science of the mind, embracing the dimension of space—the nature and substance of the mind. It can also then move to the realm of essence, our being.

Usually, concerns about emptiness and being are relegated to religious and spiritual teachings and schools. Most spiritual teachings point toward the phenomenon of space since the emptiness and freedom is seen to be needed for the life of essence. The goal of these techniques and practices is a fundamental change, a revolutionary transformation, a going beyond the self. A change of identity is sought—from that of the personality to that of Being.

However, in this study, we see that this division between psychology and religion is not real but artificial and superficial. Space, emptiness of self, can arise and can be integrated into the sense of self by dealing with psychological questions. The world view of the psychologist simply needs to expand to include the dimension of space. And, as we have seen, this is not only possible but, compared with the traditional methods of spiritual schools for "emptying" the self, it is easy.

We have shown that a psychodynamic method can lead to space because it can and usually does lead to the castration question, and from there it is only a short and simple step to space. The state of feeling castrated must be allowed and experienced. It is not really castration; the sense of castration is merely a judgment, an association, and a reaction to the state. It is merely the experience of the genital hole, the emptiness which results from the inability to experience space. If the genital hole is allowed, experienced and understood, space arises, as we have seen in our case histories. This is thoroughly documented, and can be easily demonstrated.

In psychotherapy, patients or students sometimes spend a tremendous amount of time dealing with their feelings of lack, and with their fears and defenses. The analyst can spend much time analyzing all the associations and childhood experiences relating to these feelings. The personality is full of such memories, associations, and reactions, so there appears to be a lot of understanding. But there is generally no fundamental change.

With the method we are introducing here, we can go directly to the empty hole in the unconscious self-image. Instead of analyzing and understanding every association and reaction to this lack, we can cut directly into all of them—they are only later accumulated images functioning as a veil—and go to the central experience, that of the genital hole. The associations and reactions to the hole are infinite; the student can try to understand why he feels passive, why he feels weak, why he is afraid of losing his strength, and so on, by connecting them to childhood experience. And of course when the genital hole is being dealt with directly, some of these associations do come up. However, they are not the point.

The individual feels worthless, for instance, not because he or she was treated badly and not valued in the past. The worthlessness is maintained in the present by the deficient emptiness, which is due to a loss of an aspect of one's Being. This loss is the primary event, not the events which led to it. Understanding one's worth in terms of one's relations to others in childhood can be useful and is often necessary, but it is not what will lead to transformation. Only seeing and understanding the lack, the hole itself, will lead to transformation, to the retrieval of what was lost.

Seeing and experiencing the empty hole will shed light on all the reactions and associations at once, and put them within a unified perspective. The feeling of weakness, of passivity, of inferiority, of dependency, of castration, and the defenses against all of these, like feelings of superiority and attempts at getting recognition and approval, are all mere reactions to the empty hole.

In this perspective, there is no psychology apart from spiritual questions. It is one field. Man is one; his psychology is not separate from his spirituality. Making a separation and a distinction is false; it leads to more falsehood or illusion. Illusion, then, leads to conflict, and to suffering.

The way to space is obvious and easy: The self-image must be uncovered and understood. All defenses against the empty hole must be recognized and understood. Phallic identifications which are used for defensive purposes must be broken down and dismantled. This leads to the experience of castration, of emptiness, of deficiency. Now identification with this state must be seen and understood. This reveals the genital hole. Experiencing this emptiness, accepting it and understanding it allows it to develop into space, the spacious nature of our mind. This freedom, this peace, then allows the unfolding of our true Being, our essence. This is a fundamental change; the very identity is shifted. This experience of emptiness which allows the unfoldment of Being is expressed beautifully in the following passage by J. Krishnamurti:

> There was no experiencer when this happened coming down the mountain, and yet the awareness of the mind was wholly different, in kind as well as in degree, from that which is not measurable. The mind was not functioning; it was alert and passive, and though cognizant of the breeze playing among the leaves, there was no movement of any kind within itself. There was no observer who measured and observed. There was only that, and that was aware of itself without measure. It had no beginning and no word. (Krishnamurti, *Commentaries on Living, Second Series*, pp. 241-242.)

As we see, space leads to Being, which is a fundamental transformation of the totality of the individual. However, we are here considering only the restricted question of the relationship between space and sexuality.

We have seen that the unconscious self-image of having a genital hole is a universal phenomenon. This means that for the majority of humanity, there is no real sexuality; the majority of humankind, normal or neurotic, is not connected and integrated with their sexuality. How can there be complete, full, and integrated sexuality, if unconsciously there is the deep and powerful threat of castration? The defenses against the hole create all kinds of deep tensions and contractions in the pelvis, which greatly hinder the flow of energies and bodily fluids in the area.

It is not only bodily fluids and energy that are hindered in the genital region; essence itself, the true substance of our being, is blocked. This is so prevalent that the average person does not know what it means to have real sexuality. The average individual is not a complete man or woman. Almost no one completely and fully experiences his or her genitals, owns them, or values them. Because full experience of the genitals would bring to consciousness the genital hole, experience of the genitals is partial, incomplete, and superficial. The average individual does not know what it's like to have integrated genitals, or to have essence flowing and filling them, so real sexuality is rarely experienced.

Some researchers have come close to an understanding of this situation. Wilhelm Reich, for instance, saw the importance of what he called "orgastic potency" for the healthy functioning of the human organism. He understood the many powerful defenses against true sexual openness and surrender. He realized how much fear there is about fully experiencing true pleasure in the genitals. He postulated, in fact, that this absence of orgastic potency (the capacity for total sexual surrender and energetic discharge) is the true energetic cause of neurosis. He writes:

> Erective and ejaculative potency are merely indispensable preconditions for orgastic potency. Orgastic potency is the capacity to surrender to the flow of biological energy, free of inhibitions; the capacity to discharge completely the dammed-up sexual excitation through involuntary, pleasurable convulsions of the body. Not a single neurotic is orgastically potent, and the character structures of the overwhelming majority of men and women are neurotic. (Wilhelm Reich, *The Function of the Orgasm*, p. 90.)

However, the orgastic potency advocated by Reich is a necessary but not sufficient condition for the development of a completely genitally free character. It is not enough that the biological energy flows into the genitals. Essence must be present in the pelvis, essence must be allowed to flow in the genitals, for the genitals to be truly integrated and full. And for this to happen, space must be allowed in the pelvic region. Otherwise the genital hole will continue to be defended against and feared. The genitals are not completely owned then, and sexuality is not fully experienced.

Reich understood that orgasm anxiety, pleasure anxiety, and castration anxiety must all be confronted and resolved for orgastic potency to be freed. However, we ask: How can there be full freedom without confronting the genital hole, without space and essence? The fact is that pleasure anxiety and castration anxiety cannot be completely resolved unless the genital hole is confronted and the essence freed. A truly sexually free individual is an essential individual, one who fully experiences his own being. There can be no true or full sexuality on the personality level. We will give a few examples in the form of case histories to illustrate this point.

We will return to Bart, who completes his narration of his experience after experiencing the genital hole:

> As I experienced the anger, my attention turned back towards my groin. I noticed that it was filling up with a whitish-colored substance, filling what was the empty space. As it became more present, I saw that the presence had density and was more silvery colored than white. As this silvery alive presence manifested more, it spread out from my groin and moved into my legs downward, and into my torso, arms, and head. In fact, it slowly spread throughout my entire body, soaking it like water in a sponge.
>
> As I allowed it to manifest and become more present, I saw that I no longer was overwhelmed with feelings of weakness and emasculation. I could now feel my entire groin area—each part, including my penis, was filled with this silvery aliveness. There was a feeling of confidence. I am a man. I am grounded in my genitals.

Bart is experiencing the activation of the essential aspect of will. It is not merely energy; it is the presence of Being in the form of will. We remember that Bart was feeling castrated and emasculated. What we see now is that this is due to the absence of true will. Without essential will, there is no confidence, no support in one's Beingness. This is experienced sexually as having no sexual confidence, as a castration. One cannot have complete and unconflicted confidence in one's sexuality without the true will. If the essential will is absent, is cut off, then there is a sense of castration regardless of how much it is defended against with identifications.

Will is not a masculine quality. Although the sense of strength and solidity in it is thought to be masculine, it actually has nothing to do with sexual differences. In fact, the presence of true will makes the man feel masculine and the woman feel feminine. Presence of true will brings a psychological sense of confidence. It is an implicit confidence; there is no questioning of one's determination or ability. Confidence manifests sexually as confidence in one's genitals, male or female. There is no sexual "stuttering." The following letter from Pamela, who was described previously in Chapter 11, illustrates this point clearly:

> At first I felt scared, my mind blank and very conscious of how you would react to whatever I said. My shoulders and back felt frozen. At the same time I felt calm and full in my belly with a feeling of determination to talk to you and be there.
>
> As the determined feeling increased and I paid attention to my solar plexus, what I thought was a knot was something different. I expected my will to be hard and brittle, but I felt light and strong.
>
> As my will got bigger, my mind was more clear, and I did not care about being so cautious about what I told you, and worrying about if you would like me.
>
> The feeling of space in my belly felt good. I did feel like a balloon, and I also felt the space around me. I liked the cozy warm feeling in my chest. The burning in my back and shoulders made me feel more space there too.
>
> What you said about believing my old image of myself still exists explains a lot. I expected to see my old caved-in posture. I felt surprised not to see it, surprised and glad. I felt the same way about the strength

of my real will making me more feminine. I thought
being feminine and strong could not go together.

Just as will infuses men with a sense of manhood and women
with a sense of femininity, softness and delicacy do the same for
both sexes. Softness, delicacy, and sweetness are culturally seen
to be feminine qualities. However, regardless of how they are
referred to, they have nothing to do with sexual differences. They
are qualities of Being, which transcend gender.

We return to a previous case, Mark, who at some point allowed
the full experience of space. We find him here in a private session where breathing and methods to move energy are used. He
is afraid, anxious. He is afraid of disappearing, of castration, of
inadequacy. As he works on tensions around the diaphragm,
belly, throat, and shoulders, the fear is released. Space starts manifesting at the top of his head. More work on the throat and shoulders brings about the descent of a beautiful essential state—delicate,
exquisite, brilliant in color, and peaceful. The exquisiteness and
brilliance descend into the body and encounter blockage at the
pelvis. Relaxing the pelvis leads to crying and a great fear of his
genitals disappearing. He is afraid of space. Accepting the space
in the pelvis allows the manifestation of the golden essence,
which we described previously. There is a feeling of softness,
sweetness, and melting in the genitals. Some issues and feelings
arise. By understanding them, Mark allows the merging golden
essence to fill the pelvis and genitals. Here he begins to feel complete, that there is nothing to be ashamed of. He feels a true pride
in his manly genitals.

In the following case we see the transition from phallic identification, to the genital hole and then to essence. There is a
movement from being a woman with a penis, to being a woman
with no genitals, and finally to being a woman with a vagina.

Carla, a woman in her early thirties, allows herself to let go
of her identification with having a penis and to feel feminine,
maybe for the first time in her life. She begins her private session
feeling angry, wanting to growl, but feels it is gross. She feels her

father will disapprove, but the feeling is transferred onto me. Going through some feelings of shame, growling, and expressing her anger, she finally discovers what her anger is all about. She feels that she is nothing if she is not a boy. She cries bitterly. She starts feeling nothing, an empty hole in the pelvis.

Here she tries to harden the genital area. She wants to make a penis, to bring back the hardness that makes her feel she has a penis, but she cannot do it. She has seen through this defense many times. She starts feeling vulnerable, defenseless, and scared in the genitals. Slowly she accepts the hole. It feels empty and quiet. It expands into a feeling of spaciousness, looseness.

Here, a certain softness manifests in the emptiness of the pelvis. It feels fluffy, like cotton candy. She sees it as an alive, pink presence. It feels like a light and fluffy lovingness, soft and sweet, in the genitals. She gets scared again and starts tensing her shoulders. We do more work on her fear and the tensions in her shoulders. She becomes aware of a specific fear in the pelvis, a fear of pleasurable sensation, what Reich calls pleasure anxiety. Understanding this, she starts feeling the pleasure in the presence of lovingness—the fluffy, soft feelings—in her genitals. She feels her pelvis as soft, sweetly pleasurable, melting like cotton candy into rivers of pleasure. She feels deeply feminine.

The feeling of ugliness many women have, regardless of how beautiful they are, is largely a result of rejecting their genitals. They believe that their genitals are ugly. In the following case we can see why some women believe that they or their genitals are ugly.

Linda is a young woman with beauty and proportionate form. She has been judging herself, hating herself, keeping a distance from men, hating them, exhibiting castrating behavior. At the same time, she expects judgment and rejection. We see this expectation of rejection in the way she starts her letter, which describes her experience of working on issues with me in the setting of a Work group.

> I wanted to talk to you on group night because it seems like so many things are going on in my life that I need to experience more fully. I got really scared that

there would not be enough time or that I would once again allow myself to be shelved, but it didn't happen.

Speaking to you reminded me experientially and mentally how much I tend to overlook the beauty in me and dwell on the deficiencies. I felt it was okay to let out some of the ugliness I feel inside, the resentment, the hatred, the guardedness, because I don't want to keep it all inside any more.

Experiencing the emptiness and having it be filled with precious nectars was wonderful. It made me love and appreciate my own beauty, made me feel like my pelvis was validated instead of always being under attack. It made me feel that the beauty, the fullness, the value, are all inside me, and I do not have to believe that a man or having a baby would give me those things. I felt calm, whole, and expanded.

The sense of ugliness was due to the presence of hurt, anger and hatred in the genitals. The sense of ugliness was not actually about the genitals, but about the negativity accumulated in them and in relation to them. When the emotions were erased by space, the genitals were immediately filled with the nectar-like juices of essence. This thick, syrupy, sweet and melting presence of essence is what makes one's genitals one's own. It is the delightfully alive essence engorging the pelvis with value, love, and preciousness. This allowed her to see the beauty, the real beauty, not only of her form, but of her Beingness, her true nature.

Complete sexuality, as we see, is not concerned only with sex or with intercourse. Intercourse is only one expression of sexuality. Sexuality is part of our basic nature. It is the true acceptance and integration of our bodies and genitals; it is free and unconflicted presence in the pelvis. It is our being, our essence, allowed to exist and flow in our pelvis, to engorge our genitals. It is the experience of ourselves as pleasure, as delight, as beauty, as value.

When the genital hole is allowed and understood, space arises. Space eliminates our defenses, our identification with personality. Then essence unfolds and flowers in its various beautiful manifestations. Filling and bathing our sexual area, this essence allows us to feel rooted and grounded in this beauty, this certainty, and this preciousness. Our sexuality is our relatedness, our grounding in Being. Essence is no more an idea, a concept, a feeling. It becomes our grounding in pleasure. We experience our nature as pure, unadulterated pleasure and preciousness.

This rootedness and grounding occurs only when we accept completely and fully our genitals—the man his penis and the woman her vagina. Our sex becomes our rootedness in reality. Our physical reality is completely supported then, completely integrated with our true nature. Sexuality is not only for intercourse, is not only for reproduction. It is the grounding of our Beingness.

CHAPTER FIFTEEN

Space and Inner Change

I n both depth psychology and spiritual teachings, a vital issue
that remains largely unclear is that of change, of inner change
in particular. The question of what leads to change is unre-
solved; there is no general agreement on the crucial factors con-
tributing to inner transformation. The debate about what leads to
psychic change is still going on in depth psychology, and the various spiritual teachings attribute inner transformation to different,
and sometimes contradictory, factors.

We will discuss here the arising of space as a crucial step in
the process of change and inner transformation. According to our
observations, the arising of space always precedes change. This
step is only rarely mentioned or specifically acknowledged in psychological circles. Some of the spiritual teachings acknowledge it,
refer to it, and sometimes describe it, but usually only from the
most basic and general perspective. As the material in this book
indicates, we see the subject of space as crucial in these matters

and thus deserving more specific and detailed study and understanding.

To begin with, inner change must involve a change in self-image. Otherwise the change is either temporary or it is no change at all, hidden behind a new form of the old. We discussed this point earlier, when we referred to the fact that a person who has a self-image of being weak will not feel strong or behave in a strong way unless the self-image of weakness is either changed or eliminated. For this individual to allow strength, some of his psychic boundaries will have to change or be dissolved.

Some spiritual teachings, especially those belonging to the "sudden" schools of realization, assert that change can happen only if there is no self-image at all. Only then will reality or essence manifest. The assertion is that anything less will be merely a change in self-image, which is not a significant or radical transformation.

Although this experience of total, basic change does occur and has its own logic, nevertheless it does not eliminate the possibility of other kinds of significant change. It is true that these will be changes in self-image, but this can be accompanied by deeper changes, particularly changes in the self-image which allow for the perception and realization of Being or essence in its various manifestations. This was apparent in some of our case histories.

So the most radical change, that of complete dissolution of the self-image which leads to the most radical spiritual rebirth, we will still consider a change in self-image. Self-image can change through a change in some of its boundaries. This happens through the dissolution of those boundaries. And thus the most radical change will be the complete dissolution of all boundaries in the mind.

So we see that change always involves a change in self-image; it also involves many other things, such as changes in perception, in attitude, in emotional state, in state of Being, in action, and so on. As we discussed before, self-image determines these factors of experience. In the process of change a person will often have reactions that seem to involve not more spaciousness but a more contracted self-image. This is generally a previously unconscious self-image which is made conscious by the action of space dissolving the more superficial self-image which was covering up and defending against the deeper one and its associated affects. For example, a man's self-image as brave and independent might dissolve to reveal a fearful, dependent image of a little boy, and this might dominate his experience for a while. But when a person is consistently working toward the truth, the self-image will become more and more spacious because space is the true nature of mind.

Many factors can lead to change in self-image. Most of the studies about the process of change involve determining the factors which lead to such changes. Some say it is awareness. Some say it is understanding. Some say it is love or surrender. Some say it is necessity. Some say it is conditioning. Some say it is will and action. Some say it is grace. And so on.

Although the debate goes on about which factors or combination of factors lead to change, what we are concerned with here is the understanding that, whatever factors lead to it, change in self-image is necessary for change. Our concern is with how the self-image changes, with what affects the boundaries of the self-image at moments of transformation. What is the process of change, the dissolution of self-boundaries? Understanding clearly this step in change can greatly contribute to understanding the factors that lead to it.

We have already shown that the self-boundaries which form self-image are boundaries that bound space. They structuralize space. We have seen that the dissolution of boundaries leads to the freeing of space, and can be seen as the same phenomenon as the emergence of space. Space always manifests in one's consciousness as the self-boundaries disintegrate. We can say either that space melts away boundaries or that dissolution of boundaries allows space to manifest. It is one phenomenon. The dissolution of boundaries cannot be separated from the emergence of space.

So here we see the role of space in inner change: There is no lasting change without a change in self-image, there is no change in self-image without a dissolution of self-boundaries, and there is no dissolution of boundaries without the action of space.

This is a crucial understanding lacking in most circles concerned with effecting changes in the mind or psyche. It establishes that the personality (which is determined by the self-image) cannot change itself. Only space can change it. All the personality can do, or not do, is whatever is necessary for it to be in the condition in which space can manifest and act on its boundaries.

This perspective is understood by many of the genuine spiritual teachings. They assert that the self cannot do anything to change itself or its reality. Conditioning can lead only to conditioning. The self or ego can only stop trying, stop doing, stop acting. Then the transformation occurs. This understanding is usually not as detailed as the one we are introducing here. These teachings usually see the process of radical change as giving up doing anything to change one's inner state. This then precipitates the perception of emptiness. This emptiness may then allow the experience of Being or essence. The importance of space or emptiness is seen by these teachings as a critical factor in spiritual transformation, the turning point towards spiritual rebirth and essential realization.

We can see then the relevance of the action of space to dissolve boundaries of the self-image to our statement that change and transformation can happen in increments. Changes in self-image are lasting changes, transformations which change one's relationship to Being and reality. The discovery we present here is that space is not only necessary for the most radical changes, but is also part of absolutely any change in self-image.

The following case history will illustrate this process.

Nora is a woman in her twenties who has been suffering from a negative self-image which includes weakness, indulgence, and dependence. She could not relate to another being in any assertive or strong way. She could only be passive and give in to the other. We find her here exploring the issue of asserting herself, trying to understand why she cannot contact her strength. She discovers that she is afraid that if she asserts herself, she will be rejected. However, the interesting point here is that when she tries asserting herself she is not rejected by other people, but

finds she starts rejecting herself; she rejects her own assertive-
ness and strength.

As I speak with her, she keeps taking the position of a victim.
She will not let herself feel strong or powerful. When I encourage her to speak up she becomes quite afraid, in fact, terrified.
Exploring the fear reveals the experience of emptiness. It turns
out that whenever she tries to assert her strength, space arises to
consciousness. This fills her with terror because it means to her
that she is nothing, complete emptiness. She defends against this
fear by taking the position of being a weak and passive victim.
Understanding this helps her to tolerate the emptiness. Accepting
the emptiness, she starts feeling light, spacious and empty. Here
her voice becomes louder, her posture straightens, her head goes
up. She speaks her mind freely. She feels infused by an expansive strength and vigor.

This clear example shows that space or emptiness makes possible the ending of the old and the allowing of the new. It is the
room vacated by the old which is needed for the new to manifest. There can be no change if the old continues. Change is the
death of the old and the coming to life of the new. This is true at
all levels of psychological or spiritual change.

We stress this relation of space to change and transformation
because, first, psychologists are not aware of this phenomenon,
and second, because spiritual teachings indicate that emptiness is
important only for the most radical of transformations. From the
perspective we have developed here, we can see that changes in
self-image always involve space; the smaller changes are those seen
as psychological, the deeper ones are those seen as spiritual.

We are focusing here on changes in the self-image as allowed
by the arising of space, and we maintain that the self-image is in
some sense the central point in the person's object world as constituted by the set of self-images, related object images and affects
between them. However, it is clear that the process of transformation we are describing involves changes not only in the self-
image but in the object-images and affects as well—in short, in
the person's entire world view and perceptual experience. When

107

people who are in psychotherapy are able to become more objective about the external world, they see the objects in their world, especially other people, in an entirely new way. In spiritual practice, the dissolution of boundaries on deep levels of the self-image allows profound, revolutionary changes in the perception of the true nature of the world.

Clearly, we are not asserting here that whenever one undergoes a real change, space is fully and consciously experienced. Sometimes the perception of space is clear and full, as in the example above. Other times, as we saw in earlier examples, space emerges but is not directly or clearly perceived. When space is affecting the structure but is not perceived, a person might feel dizzy or vaguely anxious. It requires some refinement of perception for an individual to perceive space in usual psychological changes, because at such times it rarely manifests completely or fully. As changes become deeper and more fundamental, space becomes more obvious and is experienced more fully.

In the final part of this book, "The Grades of Emptiness," we will see how the various depths and layers of the self or psychological identity are related to the various grades of space. From that it is easy to see that change is a change in identity. The ultimate and most radical change of identity is the dissolution of the psychological identity, or the dissolution of the identification with it. This may lead to a shift of identity from the personality to essence or Being. This is what is called spiritual rebirth or awakening.

PART THREE

The Void:
Expansion or Deficiency

CHAPTER SIXTEEN

Deficient Emptiness

We have used and emphasized the term "space" instead of "emptiness" partly to avoid confusing the experience of the void as the openness, clarity and freedom of the fundamental nature of the mind with the experience of psychological deficiency that is often termed "emptiness." Some confusion or questioning is, nevertheless, bound to arise in the minds of some readers. Therefore, we must make clear and explicit the difference between the experience of space as we have discussed it and the experience of emptiness in the normal, everyday, psychological usage of the term. We will then describe the relationship between these two experiences.

The term "emptiness" is usually used in Western languages to refer to states of inner deficiency, impoverishment, and depletion. When a person says he feels empty it is usually understood that he is referring to a painful and undesirable state, that he is feeling a lack of inner richness and profundity. Psychological emptiness is also related to depression, lack of vitality, and lack of meaning.

This sense of emptiness was highlighted by the existentialist philosophers who made it an object of study and saw it as a prevalent condition of modern man. It became connected to "nothingness," to the lack of significance and meaning, and to the state of alienation, existential suffering and anxiety (angst). William Barrett, in his book, *Irrational Man*, discussing the question of Nothingness in Heidegger's philosophy writes:

> Anxiety is not fear, being afraid of this or that definite object, but the uncanny feeling of being afraid of nothing at all. It is precisely Nothingness that makes itself present and felt as the object of our dread. The first time this fundamental human experience was described was by Kierkegaard in his concept of Dread, but there it was done only briefly, in passing; Heidegger has greatly expanded and deepened Kierkegaard's insight. . . . In Heidegger, Nothingness is a presence within our own Being, always there, in the inner quaking that goes on beneath the calm surface of our preoccupation with things. Anxiety before Nothingness has many modalities and guises: now trembling and creative, now panicky and destructive; but always it is as inseparable from ourselves as our own breathing because anxiety is our existence itself in its radical insecurity. (William Barrett, *Irrational Man*, p. 226–227.)

In the same study of existentialism, Professor Barrett writes:

> What cannot man do! He has greater power now than Prometheus or Icarus or any of those daring mythical heroes who were later to succumb to the disaster of pride. But if an observer from Mars were to turn his attention from these external appurtenances of power to the shape of man as revealed in our novels, plays, painting, and sculpture, he would find there a creature full of holes and gaps, faceless, riddled with doubts and negations, starkly finite. (Barrett, *op. cit.*, p. 65.)

The existentialist interest in emptiness as a fundamental condition of man might not be of much concern to most individuals; however, the subjective experience of emptiness is something that is commonly and frequently experienced and acknowledged. It is usually felt in a very general and vague way. An individual might feel, "My life is empty, I don't feel any richness in it." Another might experience it more inwardly: "I feel dry, empty. I am not interested or enthusiastic about anything." Sometimes the feeling becomes more philosophical: "What is the meaning of life? I don't see the point of everything."

This condition of emptiness, seen as depletion, alienation, and meaninglessness, is painfully apparent to the psychological or psychiatric helper who is treating patients suffering from the so-called severe pathologies. In fact, emptiness in the deficient sense is taken by many as one of the signs or symptoms of such disturbances as psychoses, borderline conditions, narcissistic disorders, character disorders, and schizoid phenomena. We encounter in these mental disorders experiences of, or fears of, experiencing emptiness, nothingness, hollowness, disintegration, fragmentation, dissolution, disappearing, annihilation and so on.

These states are not always vague and in the background:

> Thus a young woman of nineteen who was chronically agoraphobic and experienced serious attacks of depersonalization if she went out even with her own family, said, "I get frighteningly claustrophobic in a big store and want to rush out." It appeared that what actually happened was that she would feel overwhelmed and helpless in the midst of the big crowd of shoppers and before the fear could develop she would undergo an immediate and involuntary schizoid withdrawal. She said, "I suddenly feel a lack of contact with everybody and everything around and I feel I'm disappearing in the midst of everything." (Harry Guntrip, *Schizoid Phenomena, Object-Relations, and the Self,* p. 20.)

Guntrip continues with another example:

The following case of a young married man, a scientist working on technical problems of communication devices, shows how this sense of isolation and the accompanying feeling of emptiness of personality, can suffuse waking consciousness. After some fifty sessions, he said: "This last two weeks I've been drained of any initiative, frightened. I feel in an empty hole, nothing there. In dreams I feel to be drawn into a vacuum. There's no real foundation for my personality. I am living on the surface. I think I don't feel real. As a child I used to cry: 'Nobody cares for me.'" Then he had to go to London on business and reported, "I felt lonely there, couldn't make any contacts. I felt inferior, not qualified. I feel I couldn't attempt sexual intercourse. I haven't the status of an adult: I feel hollow, empty, and don't know what kind of person I am." (Guntrip, *Ibid.,* p. 219.)

Harry Guntrip refers to this phenomenon as schizoid. Alice Miller, writing about individuals suffering from narcissistic personality disorder, says:

In everything they undertake they do well and often excellently; they are admired and envied; they are successful whenever they care to be—but all to no avail. Behind all this lurks depression, the feeling of emptiness and self-alienation, and a sense that their life has no meaning. (Alice Miller, *Prisoners of Childhood*, p. 6.)

Heinz Kohut, in a discussion of a case of narcissistic disturbance, writes:

Mr. B. had been in analysis with a colleague (a woman) for three months. The patient, a college instructor in his late twenties, had sought analysis ostensibly because of sexual disturbances and the breakup of his marriage. Despite the seemingly circumscribed nature of his presenting symptoms, however, he suffered from a vague and widespread personality disturbance, experienced alternately as severe states of tension and as a feeling of painful emptiness, both at the borderline of physical and psychological experience. (Heinz Kohut, *The Analysis of the Self,* p. 126.)

Otto Kernberg makes "The Subjective Experience of Emptiness" a chapter in his book, *Borderline Conditions and Pathological Narcissism.* Writing about deficient emptiness, he clarifies how its experience differs in quality according to the predominant pathology:

> There are patients who describe a painful and disturbing subjective experience which they frequently refer to as a feeling of emptiness. In typical cases, it is as if this emptiness were their basic modality of subjective experience from which they attempt to escape by engagement in many activities or in frantic social interactions, by the ingestion of drugs or alcohol, or by attempts to obtain instinctual gratifications through sex, aggression, food, or compulsive activities that reduce their focusing on their inner experience. Other patients, in contrast, seem to succumb to this experience of emptiness and to acquire what might be described as a mechanical style of life—going through the motions of daily activities with a deadening sense of unreality or a blurring of any subjective experience, so that they seem to merge, so to speak, with whatever immediate inanimate or human environment surrounds them.
>
> The subjective experience of emptiness might take various forms. Some patients with chronic neurotic depression or depressive personality structures present this subjective experience only intermittently, and describe it in sharp contrast to other types of subjective experience. For them, periods in which they feel empty are characterized by a sense of loss of contact with other people, who now appear distant, unavailable, or mechanical, which they themselves feel similarly. Life no longer seems to make sense, there is no hope for any future gratification or happiness, there is nothing to search for, long for, or aspire to. . . .
>
> Other patients, that is, many patients with schizoid personality structure, may experience emptiness as an

innate quality that makes them different from other people; in contrast to others, they cannot feel anything. . . . For such schizoid patients, the experience of emptiness may be less painful than for depressed patients because there is less of a contrast between periods in which they feel empty and other times in which they would have emotional relationships with others. An internal sense of drifting, of subjective unreality, and of a soothing quality derived from this unreality, makes the experience of emptiness more tolerable to schizoid patients. . . .

There are still other patients whose experience of emptiness is a major aspect of their psychopathology; patients with narcissistic personality structures—that is, those who present the development of pathological narcissism characterized by the establishment of a pathological, grandiose self and a serious deterioration of all their internalized object relations. In contrast to the depressive and schizoid patients mentioned before, these narcissistic patients' experience of emptiness is characterized by the addition of strong feelings of boredom and restlessness. (Otto Kernberg, *Borderline Conditions and Pathological Narcissism*, pp. 213-217.)

CHAPTER SEVENTEEN

Space and
Deficient Emptiness

We see that the experience of emptiness is well known and well documented. It is familiar to the ordinary individual, the novelist, the artist, the philosopher, and the psychotherapist. However, it is almost always known as a deficient and painful subjective state.

The experience of emptiness as space, however, as illustrated in the preceding case histories, is seen to be far from deficient; it is seen and felt as an experience of lightness, freedom, clarity, and health. The void as space is experienced as empty of the sense of deficiency; there is no deficiency in self-esteem, sense of reality, or sense of self.

The feeling of space is definitely not a sense of richness, fullness, solidity, substance, or presence. However, there is no feeling of lacking or missing these qualities. Space is experienced as complete, as not needing anything. It is experienced as having its own value. It is the light and expansive sense of no burden, no heaviness, no tension, and no mental anguish.

We see then that there are two experiences of emptiness: one spacious and liberating, and the other deficient and depressive. The subjective experience is definitely different and distinct for each of these kinds of emptiness. The presence of these two types of experience of emptiness could lead to much confusion and mis-understanding, especially when one reads the literature of exis-tentialism or psychoanalysis and then contrasts it with the literature of Far Eastern philosophies and religions. One is liable to think that they are discussing the same emptiness, as we see in the fol-lowing passage by Professor W. Barrett:

> As a matter of fact, human moods and reactions to the encounter with Nothingness vary considerably from person to person, and from culture to culture. The Chinese Taoists found the Great Void tranquilizing, peaceful, even joyful. For the Buddhists in India, the idea of Nothing evoked a mood of universal compassion for all creatures caught in the toils of an existence that is ultimately groundless. In the traditional culture of Japan the idea of Nothingness pervades the exquisite modes of aesthetic feeling displayed in painting, architecture, and even the ceremonial rituals of daily life. But Western man, up to his neck in things, objects, and the business of mastering them, recoils with anxiety from any pos-sible encounter with Nothingness and labels talk of it as 'negative'—which is to say, morally reprehensible. Clearly, then, the moods with which men react to this Nothing vary according to time, place, and cultural con-ditioning. (Barrett, *op. cit.*, p. 285.)

From our study in this book so far we see that it is not merely a matter of different reactions to emptiness, but rather of the pres-ence of two separate and distinct kinds of experience of empti-ness. The Great Void of the Taoists is not the impoverished emptiness of the schizoid, and the compassionate Nothing of the

Buddhists is definitely not the restless and angry emptiness of the narcissistically structured personality. More accurately, we can say that the subjective experience of space is felt as completely different from that of the experience of deficient emptiness, although both experiences have in common the sense of voidness. The obvious and intriguing question, then, is: are these two types of experience related, and, if so, how?

In investigating whether there is a relationship between these two types of experience, we turn towards what we already know in terms of what precipitates each.

We saw in Part I, "The Void and The Self," that the experience of space is precipitated by the dissolution of self-boundaries. And we saw that these self-boundaries—which are self-images—form the sense of identity or self.

Our confusion could become compounded when we find out that similar processes lead to the experience of deficient emptiness. In fact, it is the prevalent understanding at the present time in psychoanalysis, and specifically in object relations theory, that it is the loss or absence of self-boundaries that leads to the experience of deficient emptiness. The sense of emptiness and depletion is seen as the loss or lack of part of the psychic structure. For pathological narcissism it is seen as due to the loss or weakness of the sense of self itself. Alice Miller writes:

> What is described as depression and experienced as emptiness, futility, fear of impoverishment, and loneliness can often be recognized as the tragedy of the loss of the self, or alienation from the self, from which many suffer in our generation. (Miller, *op. cit.*, p. 30.)

The sense of self, as we have mentioned, comes about through the integration of self-representations, which are the boundaries that are dissolved in the experience of space. However, we see in Miller's description that the result of this loss of boundaries is deficient emptiness and not space.

Dr. Kernberg explains the deficient emptiness not only by the loss or weakening of the self, but also by the loss of the relationship of the self with object representations, i.e., by the loss of parts of the psychic structure:

> The subjective experience of emptiness represents a temporary or permanent loss of the normal relationship of the self with object representations, that is with the world of inner objects that fixates intrapsychically the significant experiences with others and constitutes a basic ingredient of ego identity . . . when there exists a lack of an integrated self and of normal relations of the self with integrated internal objects, a more deep-seated, chronic sense of emptiness and meaninglessness of ordinary life experience ensues. Therefore, all patients with the syndrome of identity diffusion (but not with identity crisis) present the potential for developing experiences of emptiness. This experience becomes particularly strong when active mechanisms of primitive dissociation or splitting constitute a predominant defense against intrapsychic conflict. Schizoid personalities, in whom splitting processes are particularly strong and may lead to a defensive dispersal and fragmentation of affects as well as of internal and external relationships involving the self and significant objects, present strong feelings of emptiness. In narcissistic personalities, where the normal relations between an integrated self and integrated internal objects are replaced by a pathological grandiose self and a deterioration of internal objects, the experience of emptiness is most intense and almost constant. . . . Emptiness, in short, represents a complex affect state, which reflects the rupture of the normal polarity of self and objects (the basic units of all internalized object relations). (Otto Kernberg, *Borderline Conditions and Pathological Narcissism,* pp. 219–220.)

Heinz Kohut, who contributed much to the understanding of narcissism and who calls his psychology the Psychology of the Self, does not differ significantly from Otto Kernberg and other object relations theorists in terms of how the self develops—namely, as the integration of self-representations:

On the basis of certain genetic reconstructions made during the psychoanalytic treatment of patients suffering from self-pathology, I arrived at the hypothesis that the rudiments of the nuclear self are laid down by simultaneously or consecutively occurring processes of selective inclusion and exclusion of psychological structures. (Heinz Kohut, *The Restoration of the Self*, p. 183.)

Kohut's understanding is similar to Kernberg's in terms of explaining the experience of emptiness. Instead of referring to internalized objects, he refers to self-objects (the self-object is an object that is not seen by the self as completely separate from the self), and hence emptiness could result from the loss of self-objects:

The nuclear self, in particular, is not formed via conscious encouragement and praise but by the deeply anchored responsiveness of the self-objects, which, in the last analysis is a function of the self-objects' own nuclear selves. (Kohut, *Ibid.*, p. 100.)

In the following paragraph Kohut relates the experience of emptiness to the loss of the self-object (the disturbance of the patient's relationship to the analyst, in this case):

Despite the initial vagueness of the presenting symptomatology, however, the most significant symptomatic features can usually be discerned with increasing clarity as the analysis progresses, especially as the narcissistic transference in one of its forms comes into being. The patient will describe subtly experiential, yet pervasive feelings of emptiness and depression which, in contrast to the conditions in the psychosis and borderline states, are alleviated as soon as the narcissistic transference has become established—but which become intensified when the relationship to the analyst is disturbed. The patient will attempt to let the analyst know that, at times at least, especially when the narcissistic transference has become disrupted, he has the impression that he is not fully real, or at least that his emotions are dulled. (Kohut, *The Analysis of the Self*, p. 16.)

121

We seem to be coming to an impasse. On the one hand, as we saw in our case histories, the dissolution of self-boundaries leads to the experience of space; and on the other hand, as we see in the above quotations, the dissolution of the very same elements of the personality leads to the experience of deficient emptiness. This apparent impasse, fortunately, leads us to a fresh insight that will help us in seeing whether the two kinds of emptiness are related. In fact, the sought-after resolution is already within our grasp, if we just look more closely at what we have learned so far.

In Chapter 14, "Space and Sexuality," we discussed the genital hole and its genesis. We also saw that for most of our subjects the experience of space is preceded by the appearance of the genital hole. The genital hole, as we have discussed, is experienced as deficient emptiness. The deficiency can be experienced as inferiority, weakness, worthlessness, castration, etc., but mainly as emptiness. We also saw that this experience of a hole or deficient emptiness is the result of the loss of contact with space—as the nature of mind—and with essence or one's being.

In fact, we have found that when the individual encounters the genital hole—which expands into a deficient emptiness—it transforms into space as soon as it is accepted and understood. There is usually fear of disintegration or disappearing as the hole approaches consciousness; a similar fear occurs in the reports of those who encounter the deficient emptiness of the schizoid or narcissistic personalities.

When the individual understands that the deficient emptiness is the same as the feeling of the absence or loss of a certain facet of Being, it automatically and spontaneously leads to the experience of space with its lightness and expansiveness.

In our case histories the deficient emptiness appears as the genital hole primarily because we were focused on the clear space, the first grade of emptiness (see Part IV). This grade of space, the clear emptiness, is the most external and so deals with the most superficial layers of the self-image, which include sexual body-image. Dealing with the deeper spaces will lead to deeper levels of deficient emptiness, similar to those of the schizoid and narcissistic structures. The emergence of these spaces can then lead to the various aspects of Being, as we have seen in the case of the merging golden love. Some case histories will illustrate this point.

Patricia is a young, single, working woman who has been involved in the author's group for over a year. She writes about her work in one meeting:

> I began to talk about the tensions I was noticing in my head. It seemed that the fatigue and spaciness were from being in my head all the time. I started to feel hot and confused about what point I was trying to make, what I was trying to work on here. I relaxed my eyes and started to feel sad and angry. I noticed a hurt feeling in my heart. I had a feeling like something was missing in my body; it felt like a sense of who I am. Then all the feelings went away and I felt empty. It felt light and pleasant. I noticed that when I took my glasses off the emptiness expanded. My body was there but it was not a boundary. The emptiness was inside and out. It was a still and pleasant feeling.

Here Patricia is clearly feeling the narcissistic hurt, due to the deficient emptiness, which is the result of the absence of the self. When the sense of emptiness was seen to be the feeling of the absence of the sense of self, space emerged, which in this case is the black space, the second grade of space.

We must also mention that although Patricia is dealing here with a narcissistic issue, she does not have what is called a narcissistic personality structure. We will return to this important point later.

The sense of the process of moving from deficiency to space is clearer in the following case of a young man struggling to establish a career and a life of his own. In the first session he reports here, we find him still in the throes of the deficiency and its painful affects. He says after the session:

> Working with you Thursday night, I came to this state of emptiness, that is comparable to a desert . . . feeling alone in a great expanse of sand, sun, and emptiness.

This feeling of being alone, and being myself is threatening to me. I feel that now as my job and business begin to prosper I see my work here with you as more threatening. I sense that I believe that I cannot be myself and have my outer world be successful and supportive.

We looked at my relationship with my mother and how she made me responsible for her feelings, and also how she did not see my feelings and refused to relate to them.

I feel like I am resisting experiencing this condition of emptiness, voidness and aloneness. It all seems extra threatening right now. The state I experienced had such a quietness to it. Although alone, the peacefulness had a soft cloud-like quality.

I also sense that I am resisting fully accepting my feelings of sadness and hurt right now, or not allowing myself to feel them. This is just as my mother taught me, "Don't feel your feelings, Nick," and how she herself acted.

I feel cold and dry, very dry, as if an essential warmth, confidence and richness is missing. My parents were so closed to accepting me, or seeing me, that I abandoned my own true qualities of fullness, warmth, and simple Beingness.

We see here the deficient emptiness that feels dry like a desert, cold and alone. We also notice Nick's difficulty in accepting it and its accompanying affects of hurt, sadness and abandonment. This, he says, is threatening to him. To accept his feelings and true qualities means being alone, because it means the loss of the internalized object-representation—his mother in childhood—and also the loss of the self-object, which is the outer world now. So he is saying that to accept the emptiness and its painful affects is tantamount to being himself without the support of the self-object. He still needs the support of the self-object for the feelings of warmth, confidence, and inner richness. This is the usual narcissistic dilemma, of either having oneself or the self-object, a dilemma that is experienced as intolerable by the self.

However, we find that the emptiness sometimes tips towards the black space, when he experiences the emptiness as peaceful and soft. After three weeks of struggling and living with these feelings he writes after a session:

> In working with you Thursday night I was afraid that I'd experience hurt and pain like I had been during the three weeks between group sessions. Instead I opened into a very expanded peaceful state. You asked me how large this space was or felt like. It felt like it went on forever, extremely expanded. I felt very empty-headed, peaceful, clear, and present. A very nonstriving kind of sense of peace pervaded.

Nick allowed himself to experience and accept the hurt and pain for three weeks. And, as he reports, this led directly to the emergence of peaceful and pleasant space. The deficient emptiness with its fears and hurts was replaced by the freeing emptiness.

Some of the examples given in Part II, in the chapter, "Space and Sexuality," illustrate the transition from space to the experience of Being. So rather than giving more case histories to illustrate the various transitions, which by now must be clear to the reader, we move forward to find a theoretical framework that will account for all of the above observations.

CHAPTER EIGHTEEN

The Genesis of
Deficient Emptiness

First we list the major findings and observations that we need to account for. From object relations theory we have the following:

i. The personality and the sense of self develop in early childhood as a result of the integration of self-representations through the process of separation-individuation.

ii. The sense of deficient emptiness, which is especially apparent in the severe mental disorders, is due to the loss or weakening of the sense of self or its relation to the internal object (or to the self-object).

From our discussion of space in this book we have the following:

iii. The development of the sense of self or identity is the same as the construction of psychological boundaries and freezing them in the openness of space. This is usually referred to, in object relations theory, as the building of psychic structures in the mind.

iv. As these boundaries, which are the specific images involved in self-representations, dissolve, a deficient emptiness arises accompanied usually by some painful affects.

v. When these affects with their sense of deficiency are understood and accepted, the deficient emptiness disappears, allowing the emergence of space as a pleasant and peaceful spaciousness.

vi. From our discussion of essence or Being we also learned that the deficient emptiness is basically the loss of contact with one's being, space being one of its aspects representing the ontological nature of mind.

We propose the following hypothesis to account for all of the above six points:

- At birth the human infant has no sense of self.
- He is Being. He is his being without knowledge or self-consciousness. There is no mental functioning yet.
- Slowly, through experiences of pleasure and pain, memory traces are retained, forming the first self-impressions (self-representations).
- As the infant starts taking himself to be this or that (this or that self-image) he separates from his sense of Being, because any image is not his being.
- As the ego-identity and sense of self develop and become stable, the contact with Being in its various aspects and qualities is mostly lost. The extent of the loss also depends on the adequacy of the environment and the infant's relation to it.
- The process of loss of contact with Being leaves a sense of deficiency, a state of deficient emptiness, as if the Being is left with many holes in it. The deficient emptiness is the state of the absence of contact with or awareness of Being.

- Space, which is the open dimension of Being, is lost in the formation of the self-image. This self-image includes the unconscious body-image of having a genital hole.
- For the normal individual, the development of the personality happens relatively smoothly. The self is highly integrated and stays stable throughout most of one's life.
- In those with mental disorders, for reasons already known in depth psychology, the development of the personality and its sense of self is incomplete, or happens with various distortions, malformations, or inadequacies.

The above hypothesis clearly takes into consideration the findings of depth psychology, especially those of object relations theory. The major point in it is the introduction of the concept of Being or essence.

We can easily deduce the following points from our hypothesis:

a. The ego structure, with its sense of identity, contains within it a deficient emptiness. This is true for any person whose identity is with self-image instead of with just Being. This includes individuals with normal, neurotic, or pathological personality structures. Clearly, this refers to virtually all human beings.

b. The extent of the sense of deficient emptiness depends on how complete the loss of contact with Being is.

c. Also, the sense of deficient emptiness depends on how vulnerable or incomplete the personality structure is. For normal and neurotic structures—where there is a stable sense of identity—the deficiency is very much unconscious and successfully defended against. For those with severe mental disorders, the weaknesses or rips in their structures expose them more readily to this deficient emptiness and the anxieties and pains accompanying it or in reaction to it.

d. Individuals with integrated personalities and a stable sense of self can tolerate confrontation with deficient emptiness much better than ones with pathological structures. There is a resiliency in the personality that is able to accommodate temporary disintegration. Partly because the well-integrated personality can tolerate some disintegration, these personalities might find themselves approaching spiritual or psychological disciplines which open one to deeper experiences. Those characters whose defenses are "thin" or in some respects inadequate might experience problems which can be seen as pathological, but often also are more open to emptiness and thus to realms of Being beyond the personality, and manifest this openness in creative endeavors such as art, philosophy, etc. This point is more of an observation, both in the field of psychotherapy and in our work, than a deduction from the hypothesis.

e. The most important point for our discussion in this book, which is an integral part of our hypothesis, is that the deficient emptiness results from the loss of contact with Being; and not from the loss of psychic structures. Being existed before the development of the psychic structure. Thus the explanation given by the above-mentioned psychoanalysts is true, but more from an observational point of view than from a genetic one. In other words, structural losses and weaknesses expose an already existing deficient emptiness, rather than generate it.

The material we have presented so far indicates clearly that in the psychodynamic process of understanding the personality, one undergoes a regression which proceeds through the following major steps:

1. Disidentifying with parts of the psychic structure leads to the experience of deficient emptiness.

2. The deficient emptiness leads to the experience of space.

3. Space leads to the awareness of Being.

The following case shows these steps clearly and illustrates the relationships between these steps as the individual regresses from one layer of the personality to a deeper one.

In this case we find Donna, whom we mentioned in Chapter 14, trying to understand her smoking habit in the hope of getting over it:

> When I worked with you Thursday night at first I experienced nervousness and fear, along with excitement. After I'd explained what had happened around my

independent attempt to understand my smoking habit, I experienced anger, sadness, and fear. I noticed feeling those things about my parents and I was trying to figure out how that all fit in. Then I felt a loss of mother that felt like a loss also in my chest. With the feeling of emptiness in my chest I felt hungry, and experienced a reflex type feeling of sucking around my mouth and jaw. The emptiness in my chest at first had a desperate quality of lack, and I felt a desperate need and longing to fill it. After I let myself feel the sucking, the emptiness stayed but I felt more at ease with it. The desperate quality went away, and it was a light emptiness, but I was still not completely comfortable with it. Then there was a burning in my sternum that radiated a sweet light fullness in my body. The fullness felt like a warm, caring pleasure, love, appreciation and contentment, all mixed together.

It is unmistakably clear in this case that the loss of part of the psychic structure—in this case the loss of the internalized object (mother) representation—exposes a deficient emptiness. It is also clear that both the mother-representation and smoking fulfill the same purpose—to fulfill the oral longing. In Donna's experience, the oral hunger is the affect accompanying the deficient emptiness; namely, the emptiness had the quality of lack. She tried to fill this lack either with smoking or with mother's image.

It is also clear in Donna's report that accepting and understanding the lack transforms the emptiness to space (from a desperate emptiness to a light emptiness).

The experience of space leads readily to the awareness of the fullness of her essence. Genetic reconstruction of this case leaves no doubt that the loss of the aspects of Being related to caring, pleasure, love and contentment (Being as nourishment) leaves a deficient emptiness that longs for fulfillment, which Donna attempts to relieve by incorporating mother's image or smoke.*

---

* For more elaborate discussion of the process of loss of Being that leads to deficient emptiness and attempts to fill it with parts of the psychic structure, see *Essence,* Chapters Three and Four, by the author. Some of the profound consequences of this process are also discussed there.

The work of understanding the self-image and abandoning it slowly, as in the case above, is not a therapeutic work, although it could have therapeutic side results. It is a work oriented towards human development and inner realization. As we see, as the process deepens, the identity slowly shifts from self-images from the past to the actual experience of Being in the present.

This has been the concern of philosophy and religion, and very seldom that of psychology. However, we see here that this process of the unfolding of human essence is psychological in nature, and can be approached through psychological means. In fact, we have shown it here as a psychodynamic process.

We must note that we are not making any statement here about this process of unfoldment as it relates to individuals with severe structural disorders. Our experience lies only with individuals possessing integrated and stable personality structures. The unfoldment is a slow process of "peeling," done in a balanced and quiet manner. The various self-images are exposed first. They then become ego-alien. Then the person lets go of them by understanding their psychodynamics. This leads to emptiness and then to Being.

It might be interesting and fruitful to investigate the severe disorders of structure using our hypothesis. The understanding of space as it relates to deficient emptiness might prove to be of some help to such individuals. However, we have to leave such study and application to the specialists who are already working on them.

Even in the case of the normal person with an integrated structure, the emergence of the deficient emptiness arouses many strong and painful emotional states, similar to the ones reported by people suffering from disorders of structure. The following report by the Indian teacher Bhagwan Rajneesh about some of the experiences leading to his final realization, is illustrative:

> My condition was one of utter darkness. It was as if I had fallen into a deep dark well. In those days I had many times dreamt that I was falling and falling and going deeper into a bottomless well. And many times I . . . awakened from a dream full of perspiration, sweating

131

profusely because the falling was endless without any ground or place anywhere to rest my feet . . . for me there was no clear path. It was all darkness. Every next step for me was in darkness—aimless and ambiguous. My condition was full of tension, insecurity and danger. (Vasant Joshi, *The Awakened One*, p. 51.)

We see Rajneesh here experiencing the deficient emptiness with its painful affects and feelings. Then, as he emerges from this state, he reports the experience of space as emptiness without the affect of deficiency:

I have recognized the fact that I am not, so I cannot depend on myself, so I cannot stand on my own ground . . . I was in . . . a bottomless abyss. But there was no fear, because there was nothing to protect. There was no fear, because there was nobody to be afraid. (Joshi, *Ibid.*, p. 61.)

It is interesting that here Rajneesh is describing a state of no self without the presence of fear, and that he ascribes the absence of fear to the absence of self. This point will be important to us later in our study of emptiness. He then continues to report the emergence of some qualities of Being:

And the last day the presence of a totally new energy, a new light and new delight, became so intense that it was almost unbearable, as if I was exploding, as if I was going mad with blissfulness. (Joshi, *Ibid.*, p. 61.)

He then describes the shift of identity to Being, an experience he calls his enlightenment:

Those three hours became the whole eternity, endless eternity. There was no time, there was no passage of time; it was the virgin reality—uncorrupted, untouchable, unmeasurable. (Joshi, *Ibid.*, p. 65.)

This last passage says something about nonconceptual reality, the ultimate space or supreme reality, Being with no self-image.

It becomes clear by now that the existentialist philosophers were actually describing a fundamental truth of the presence of emptiness at the core of the personality, although they did not differentiate between space and deficient emptiness. Professor Barrett writes:

> That man is finite is not merely a psychological characteristic of him personally or his species. Nor is he finite merely because his number of allotted years on this earth is limited. He is finite because the 'not'—negation—penetrates the very core of his existence. And whence is this 'not' derived? From Being itself. Man is finite because he lives and moves within a finite understanding of Being. (Barrett, *op. cit.*, p. 277.)

This truth, that emptiness results from the loss of Being, has been discussed by some depth psychologists. Among them the British object relations psychologist, D. W. Winnicott, came closest to our hypotheses. His hypothesis of the "true self" that is replaced or covered by the "false self" is almost the same as our understanding. He actually wrote of Being and the loss of Being, and not only about the development of ego structure. Writing on ego integration in child development, he says about the anxiety relating to deficient emptiness:

> Unthinkable anxiety has only a few varieties, each being the clue to one aspect of normal growth:
> (1) Going to pieces
> (2) Falling forever
> (3) Having no relationship to the body
> (4) Having no orientation.
> (Winnicott, *op. cit.*, p. 58.)

In fact these forms of anxiety are reported by some of the people working on inner realization. Although these anxieties are usually considered by analysts to be of a psychotic nature, they do occur in normal structures if one goes deeply into the unconscious, as in the case of Rajneesh.

In the following passage Winnicott writes clearly about the connection between the deficient emptiness (which he refers to as annihilation) and the loss of Being:

Anxiety in these early stages of parent-infant relationship relates to the threat of annihilation, and it is necessary to explain what is meant by this term.

In this place, which is characterized by the essential existence of a holding environment, the "inherited potential" is becoming itself a "continuity of being." The alternative to being is reacting, and reacting interrupts being and annihilates. Being and annihilation are the two alternatives. (Winnicott, *op. cit.*, p. 47.)

Harry Guntrip, a student of Winnicott, took his teacher's observation about Being and made it central to his object relations theory. He writes:

In absence, non-realization, or dissociation of the experience of "being" and of the possibility of it, and, along with that, incapacity for healthy natural spontaneous "doing" is the most radical clinical phenomena in analysis. Patients realize that they have been working hard all their lives busily "doing," not in a natural but a forced way, to create an illusory sense of reality as a person, a substitute for the experience of "beingness" in a solid and self-assured way that is the only basis of the self-confidence nearly all patients complain of lacking. The experience of "being" is more than the mere awareness of "existence." It involves the sense of reliable security in existence, realized both in knowing oneself as a real person, and as able to make good relationships. The experience of "being" is the beginning and basis for the realization of the potentialities in our raw human nature for developing as a "person" in personal relationships. (Harry Guntrip, *Schizoid Phenomena, Object Relations and the Self,* p. 254.)

The forced "doing" that Guntrip refers to is the activity of the self, a self that is based on identifications with self-images instead of on the experience of Being. The activity is forced because it is based on the deficient emptiness.

CHAPTER NINETEEN

Emptiness is Emptiness

An important question remains unanswered: Why, when Being or its aspect of space is lost, is what remains nothingness and not something else? In other words, why do we end up with emptiness and not another content of experience?

To answer this question we have to discuss the point at which psychodynamics touches phenomenology. We need to see how psychodynamic processes—which are processes in time—affect felt phenomena—which always involve spatially experienced objects of perception. We first consider how specifically the loss of space leads to deficient emptiness.

Space is lost as the mind takes self-image for identity. We have seen that this leads to the building of boundaries in the openness of space. The final result is that instead of the experience of Being without mental images, one ends up with a mental image for an identity. So instead of space being pervaded by Being it gets filled with a self composed of many self-representations.

Now, what is the phenomenon of space when it is filled with the self? In other words, what is the mind filled with the psychic structure? On the surface it is the usual experience of the personality with its various manifestations. But, at the core, it is the deficient emptiness.

This means that if the totality of the personality is seen objectively and graphically it looks like an empty shell; the shell is composed of many layers, each standing for a self-representation. Identifying with the shell gives the feeling of self or identity. When one ceases identifying with the shell as a whole there will emerge the experience of deficient emptiness, accompanied by the affect of the sense of no self.

The sense of being an empty shell, when it is finally perceived, is accompanied by the feeling of being fake and a sense of shame that is a reaction to the fakeness. We will not go deeper into this question of the shell—for it belongs to the study of narcissism in its relation to Being—but will content ourselves with giving a particular case history to illustrate the fact of the personality's core being the deficient emptiness.

June, a single woman in one of the helping professions, has been exploring some of her feelings of deficiency, shame, and lack of value. At some point she started experiencing a state that she described as "I am not," which is the experience of the loss of the feeling of self. She writes me about her experience of working with me in a group setting, where she experienced herself as a shell containing emptiness:

> As you were working with someone else I could hear each word that you said but could give the sentences no meaning. Then began the feeling of "I am not." I experienced some anxiety at not being able to stay with the experience.
>
> As you began to talk to me I was able to respond most of the time but sometimes could make no sense of what you said. The experience was of awareness with no "I."
>
> When you asked me what was in my chest, I felt emptiness, but the 'shell' reformed around it. We went

back and forth between shell and empty space a few times. When the shell appeared there was aversion to it. Then I experienced shame at how fake everything about me is.

You asked me to stay with the emptiness. Then love came into the chest.

Now, if our true identity, as Winnicott says, is Being, then obviously taking ourselves to be a certain image means we have a lack of knowledge or understanding about our nature. In other words it means there is ignorance about one's Being. In fact much of the personality consists of wrong ideas and beliefs about what one is, plus the emotional affects associated with them.

This content of mind obviously—since it is ignorance and lack of understanding—must cloud the clarity of the mind. It acts as an obfuscation, a dullness, a darkness which interferes with the clarity of mind. But we have seen that the nature of the mind is ultimately space. Thus this ignorance, which is mental dullness or darkness, interferes with and obscures the sharpness and clarity of space.

Space made dull and dark by the obscuring effect of ignorance is deficient emptiness.

In other words, deficient emptiness is nothing but space experienced through the filter of ignorance (which is composed of images from the past taken to define oneself, accompanied by wrong beliefs and emotions associated with the images). This explains why when the deficient emptiness is experienced it transforms into space as soon as the wrong beliefs and their accompanying emotions are seen and understood.

Of course, the ignorance has in it, connected to it, the memories of the original childhood experiences that led to the various self-images. Psychodynamic understanding removes the dullness and darkness of ignorance by shedding light on its specific content. This brings about the clarity of understanding, which dissipates the ignorance and reveals the true nature of the deficient emptiness which is immaculate space.

This argument shows that deficient emptiness is nothing but space obscured by ignorance and falsehood. It is difficult to give a more precise discussion of this point, because we are dealing with the interface of two kinds of realities: the ontological nature of the mind, and its content.

However, our discussion is based on the direct experience and observation of the phenomena involved in the transition from deficient emptiness to space. We notice that as the understanding of the beliefs and affects associated with the deficient emptiness becomes clearer and more precise, the deficient emptiness slowly and gradually lights up, lightens up, and becomes clearer and more spacious.

It is as if the ignorance and falsehood constitute a dark and subtle cloud that pervades space and makes it into a dull and heavy emptiness. When this cloud is dissipated through understanding, the true clarity and openness of space shines through.

On the other hand, if what is being dealt with is not the loss of space itself, but some other quality of Being, such as love or joy, then, as self-images are dissolved, what is left is space plus the ignorance relating to the lost aspect of Being. This ignorance comprises past self-images and associated false beliefs, ideas, and emotions relating to the loss, plus the memories of the childhood situations that led to the loss. This mental content forms something like a dark, subtle cloud which obscures the sharpness, clarity, and spaciousness of space. So we end up with a deficient emptiness. But it is a different form of deficient emptiness, because its obscuring darkness is related to an aspect of Being other than space.

For each lost aspect of Being, a different form of deficient emptiness results. These different forms can be seen as the various holes in one's being or in one's personality. Each hole is a deficient emptiness in which the feeling of deficiency manifests as an affect of the lack of a specific quality.

This explains why, when dealing with self-image, we always encounter space in the process of transformation. This is the deeper reason behind our assertion in Chapter 15, "Space and Inner Change," that change always involves the encounter with space. We also see here the basis for the rationale behind our discussion in Chapter 13, "Space and Essence": when the psychic content that resulted from the loss of a specific aspect of essence or Being is seen and understood, its obscuring effects dissipate, leading first to space and then to the emergence of the essential aspect lost.

We see that the experience of deficient emptiness—which is the interface of space and mental content—is of paramount importance, not only for understanding mental disorders, but for the process of unfolding of human potential.

Some thinkers have proposed that the experience of psychosis, or something like psychosis, is important or even essential for the process of unfolding and inner growth. What we see emerging here, however, is that it is not the experience of psychosis or mental disorder that is essential, but the experience of deficient emptiness. It is one of the essential steps towards the realization of the full human potential which is Being.

PART FOUR

The Grades of Emptiness

CHAPTER TWENTY

The Grades of Emptiness

It is clear from our discussion of the phenomenology of space
and the section on essential development that there is more
than one kind of inner space. Space or emptiness exists at
various depths of experience, or various degrees of subtlety in
identification. Each level of space is different phenomenologically
and is experienced differently. But there is always the emptiness,
always the openness. And the experience of any grade of space
is always connected to the dissolution of some boundary of the
self, or the ego's identity.

We have discussed the sense of self in terms of self-boundaries or self-image. We have seen how these boundaries which
form the sense of self actually bound the openness of empty space,
and that these boundaries function not only as partitions but also
as limiting walls.

We have not so far distinguished between the various grades
of space because it has not been directly relevant to our discussion,

and more importantly, it is not relevant to the beginning experience of space. Seeing space in its various grades and depths is a refinement and an added subtlety.

However, as one goes deeper into freeing the mind from self-boundaries, and as essence is awakened and developed, it becomes important and even necessary to distinguish between the various kinds of space. Here, the various grades or levels of space will be seen to be connected to different depths and subtleties of the sense of self or separate identity. As the boundaries of the self become subtler and more fundamental, space becomes deeper and more powerful in its annihilating influence. This process continues until one is able to experience reality with no boundaries at all, with no sense of separate identity whatsoever, with no sense of individual experience. Although this might sound fantastic, undesirable, or even frightening, it remains nonetheless the objective of spiritual (essential) development. This development is reached by some individuals, and it is experienced as the freest and most positive condition possible. It is equated with liberation and enlightenment.

Rather than going into the details of the various spaces, a discussion of which would be too subtle and hard to understand without direct experience of emptiness and its relation to self-image, we will say just a few words about the subtler spaces, putting them in their right perspective in terms of their relationship to the various depths of the sense of identity.

Again we will use Mahler's formulation of the sense of self to gain a deeper understanding of the self-boundaries on their various levels. This is not the only possible way of seeing identity at its various depths, but this perspective can help us to understand the subtle spaces in some kind of order and relationship to each other.

We will refer again to the already quoted passage from Mahler about the two kinds of body-image:

> The infant's inner sensations form the core of the self. They seem to remain the central crystallization point of the "feeling of self," around which a "sense of identity" will become established (Greenacre, 1958;

Mahler, 1958; Rose, 1964, 1966). The sensoriperceptive organ—the "peripheral rind of the ego," as Freud called it—contributes mainly to the self's demarcation from the object world. The two kinds of intrapsychic structures together form the framework for self-orientation (Spiegel, 1959). (Margaret Mahler, *op. cit.*, p. 35.)

Here, Mahler shows the acuteness of her observation and the creativity of her formulation. In seeing the various grades of space, we will appreciate how accurate this formulation is. She is stating here that there are two kinds of body-image, or in her words, "the body ego contains two kinds of self-representations." One body-image is related to the outside, in relation to the external environment. It includes the shape, the contours, the size, the texture, etc. of the body. The other body-image is related to the inside; its boundaries are in relation to the inner environment. It includes inner body and organ sensation.

The first body-image contributes to the self-image, especially in its demarcation from the outside. It contributes to the sense of separateness of the self. The second body-image contributes to the self-boundaries more in terms of a feeling of self, and not as much to the sense of separateness. Of course, the sense of demarcation and separateness from the outside contributes, in turn, to this feeling of self. The sense of separateness is, in fact, an important aspect of the sense of identity. Both self-images (or as Mahler calls them above, "intrapsychic structures") ultimately generate, and in fact form, the sense of identity.

So we see here that the sense of self has in it two kinds of self-image (two kinds of self-representations) and two kinds of body-image, forming the nuclei of the self-images. We have seen that this multiplicity is a result of the body having two sets of boundaries, inner and outer.

Another factor leading to this multiplicity or layering of self-representations is the process by which this sense of self is developed. We have seen that the ego-identity develops as a result of the separation-individuation process, and also that this process has two distinct lines of development—separation and individuation.

The line of development of separation is mainly related to the external body-image and its corresponding self-image. The line of individuation is connected primarily to the internal body-image and its corresponding self-image. Of course there is no clear-cut distinction between the various images, and no clear linear and causal connection. This whole picture of the personality is general and approximate. It is however, sufficient for our understanding of the various grades of emptiness.

To summarize, we have delineated the following parts of the self-boundaries:

    i. the external self-image

    ii. the internal self-image

    iii. the external body-image, which is the nucleus of the external self-image

    iv. the internal body-image, which is the nucleus of internal self-image.

The grades of space, we will observe, are each connected generally with one of these sets of boundaries. The first kind of space, for instance, acts to dissolve the boundaries of the external self-image. However, it will not have what is needed to penetrate more deeply to affect the deeper sets of boundaries. However, other spaces may emerge, each capable of penetrating more deeply into the subtle boundaries of the self.

So we see that although the first grade of space, for instance, might be present, there can still be a sense of identity; but now the sense of identity is connected to the deeper three sets of boundaries. The first space cannot act on these subtler boundaries. The balance of this chapter will describe the various grades or levels of space.

    i. *Clear space.* This is the space we have mainly described so far in this book: the clear, empty, and light spaciousness. It is related generally to the external self-image, which is the closest set of boundaries to our normal consciousness.

    ii. *Black space.* This is an empty, light, but black spaciousness. Its phenomenological relation to the clear space is like the relation of night to day. It is generally related to the internal self-image, which is usually deeper and more difficult to surrender. The loss of this deeper boundary is usually experienced as a loss of identity. While for the clear space a commonly associated fear is one of disintegration, for this black space, the fear is of not knowing who one is.

As the black space arises, there is a sense initially of a lack of orientation, which produces much anxiety. But if the individual allows the disorientation, and surrenders the sense of self, after a while the black empty space will be experienced as containing a sense of depth, silence and peace.

iii. *Clear dense space.* Dealing with the boundaries of the external body image will lead to a clear kind of space, but different from the above clear space in that it will paradoxically be experienced as full. It will have a fullness and a presence, like the body. But at the same time it will be space. It is a compact and dense space, experienced at the same time as openness. But the openness is immense and powerful.

The influence of this clear dense space is not exactly the dissolution of physical boundaries; more exactly, the experience of this space allows the perception that the boundaries of the body are themselves space, and hence are not real boundaries.

It is not possible to conceive of this dense (full) space without experiencing it. The mind can only conceive of space that is similar to physical space, and this particular space has characteristics physical space does not have.

iv. *Black dense space.* Dealing with the boundaries of the internal body image will precipitate the experience of a dense space like the preceding one, but black instead of clear. This space arises when the individual lets go of the sense of identity stemming from inner bodily sensations.

This sense of identity stems not only from the quality or kind of inner sensations of the body, but more importantly from the mere presence of these sensations and impressions. In other words, the identity here is very much connected with the mere presence of the body. This identity is with the body. The loss of this set of boundaries will usually bring the fear of loss of the body itself. So in dealing with this particular set of boundaries, the individual comes across the fear of death.

In fact, the fear of death is encountered in all the black spaces. The personality does not usually differentiate itself from the body when feelings about death are involved.

These first four levels of space then can be seen to relate to the four kinds of self-image we discussed above. As an individual goes through the process of dissolving these self-images, these spaces will arise, although there is no absolute order in which these kinds of self-image and space might be dealt with in such a process. Much more detailed experience and information regarding these spaces and the process of dissolution of boundaries is available; this chapter is meant only as the briefest of descriptions of these matters.

In addition to these four spaces, there are others, subtler in nature and connected to the sense of identity in the deeper realms of experience and the subtler structures of the mind.

v. *Annihilation space.* This is a black, empty space encountered at a very subtle level of identity, the sense of identity which stems from the experience of existence. Here we are not dealing with boundaries of any image; we are dealing with the identity itself, the actual feeling of existence. Identity itself, both ego-identity and essential identity (identification with Being), is annihilated here in this space.

As this space arises, the individual encounters fears of death, of disappearing, of annihilation, of nonexistence. This space is actually the experience of nonexistence, of complete extinction of self, of cessation. The cessation can be so deep that even awareness and consciousness cease for a time. The person here is not only afraid of the death of the body, but is also afraid that his mind will cease to exist. And this cessation of mind is exactly the experience of this space.

This space, although it arouses the greatest terror, is experienced as the greatest peace. The calm, the silence, the peace, is complete, total. It is utter relief. When you are no more, then there is no more suffering. Cessation and nonexistence is blissful peace.

This space is the blackest. It is so deep and black that even consciousness is annihilated. One enters deepening blackness, so that after a while one cannot see anything; one is swallowed in the abyss.

vi. *The Void.* Even the annihilation space is experienced, and hence there is a boundary. In other words, it is an individual experience. The annihilation is still related to oneself. The sense of individual experience remains, in a very subtle sense, as the annihilation of self. The experience is still self-centered, self-related. The annihilation happens to somebody, to oneself.

The dissolution of this subtle boundary of individual experience leads to a yet deeper and more open space, an utterly empty space. This space is complete and total emptiness. It is the emptiness which eliminates separating boundaries.

There is no more a sense of individual experience. There is nobody there experiencing the emptiness. At this level, there is no difference between awareness and emptiness.

Again, this space cannot be conceived by the mind. The mind cannot conceive of experience which is not an individual experience. According to the mind, experience always belongs to someone, to a self, to an individual. Only the taste of this experience can give an understanding of this space. In this space, experience is completely open. There is freedom without the notion of freedom.

Of course, one can experience several spaces at the same time, depending on the boundaries being dissolved. In fact, this happens frequently. But it takes a great perceptivity and subtle discrimination for an individual to be aware of all the spaces.

The above list does not describe all possible spaces; these are only the major categories. The refinement and subtlety can go on further, but these refinements are relevant only to those involved in the experience.

As the process of the deepening dissolution of boundaries and the related experiences of space goes on (which we mentioned above need follow no absolute sequence), it usually happens that all manner of experiences and realizations not directly involving space intervene. We refer particularly to the experience of essence in its various aspects and dimensions. In fact, the experience of essence contributes greatly to the deepening experience of space. Without the invaluable presence of essence, it is very difficult, almost impossible, to tolerate the loss of the deeper boundaries. The experience of ego death and annihilation is too frightening to allow without the experience of a reality beyond the ego, the reality of Being, our true essence.

And in turn, the realization of emptiness in its various grades contributes to the discovery and development of essence, and ultimately to its actualization as the real life.

The dimension of space deepens and opens up as the realm of Being deepens and expands. The ultimate experience of space is beyond all concepts, even the concepts of space and Being. This is the experience of nonconceptual reality, the ground of all existence. It cannot even be called an experience. We can call it the Ultimate Space or the Supreme Reality as long as we remember that such concepts fail to reach it. It is the ultimate mystery, where mind cannot go.

This ultimate reality, beyond all concepts, is seen then to be one's true identity, one's ultimate self. It is knowing oneself without self-image. It is knowing oneself by being oneself. This is self-realization.

APPENDIX

Space, Representations and Being

The realization and understanding of space is necessary for the perception of objective reality—what we will call objective perception. Objective perception means perceiving reality, all that confronts our awareness, as it is. It is a matter of seeing things as they are, rather than seeing them from a certain point of view or position. So by objective we do not mean the scientific positivist sense, in which objective means what exists physically outside us rather than in the mind. We also do not mean objective in the sense of not being emotional, or not being experiential. We mean seeing things, seeing internal or external things, as they are, instead of subjectively. Subjective is the antithesis; it means according to our positions, feelings, filters, beliefs and attitudes. So objective perception means pure perception, free from all positions, bias, filters, conflicts, intentions, etc. It is perceiving whatever it is without any obscuration or intermediacy, so we see it just the way it is in itself.

The way the conventional or ego self experiences things, the way we ordinarily perceive reality, the way we perceive each other, the way we feel, sense, touch, and see are generally speaking not objective. Our normal, everyday perception is filtered through a great many obscurations. An important part of spiritual work, in a sense the point of it—that which is sufficient to take us the whole way on any path—is to experience things objectively: to experience, feel, sense, taste and see objectively. When this happens we say we are experiencing Reality. So, what is called spiritual realization, which is the same as experiencing Reality, does not mean having supernatural experiences.

The primary way we lose our objectivity has to do with representations. To experience reality as it is means to apprehend it without our representations of it. In other words, the main reason we don't experience things objectively is that we look at reality through our representations of it. We take our ideas of it, beliefs about it, images of it, memories of it, etc. as describing it, and then look at reality through these filters.

We are using the word "representation" in the general sense of the word, not in the technical, psychoanalytic sense like in self- or object representations. Whenever we need to think, talk, or communicate with others, we need to represent reality. We cannot speak without representing. In verbal representation we take a string of words or a string of letters to represent some percept. Representation makes it possible for us think and communicate verbally, and so, of course, it is important and necessary.

And generally speaking, as long as we are using our representations of reality for thinking and communicatiing about reality, there is no problem. However, we end up using representations not only for thinking and communicating about reality, but also for perceiving it. We end up experiencing reality through the representations we have learned or constructed. For instance, we have the representation of the sun. Most people rarely look at the sun without their representation of it—their image of the sun and the word "sun," which brings with it memories about the sun and what the sun means. The perception of the sun becomes laden with the concept "sun," our scientific knowledge about it, our previous experiences of it, our associations to the representation, and so on. In fact, carried by our memory, all of our past experience and knowledge related to the representation of sun comes to the fore in our experience of the sun.

The representation of the sun is basically a conceptualization of a certain part of how things appear to us at certain times. Reality appears to awareness discriminated in various kinds of colors, forms and shapes. We carve out a certain form or a certain pattern and give it a name, a picture. This becomes a representation, which we take thenceforth to mean that there is really something like this that exists as an object. We end up looking at this pattern of appearance through the filter of the concept "sun."

There has been a great deal of discussion, philosophical and spiritual, about representational thinking. Spiritual teachings emphasize how representational thinking is a problem. Our understanding here is not that representational thinking is the problem, but that the problem is using representations for perception. To think and speak we have to use representations, but that by itself does not necessarily distort reality. However, when our representations completely determine the ways in which we perceive reality then that becomes a specific problem.

An important aspect of any spiritual teaching is to see the truth about one's own nature. For this reason we must explore the ways in which we perceive and experience ourselves. This work involves making conscious the representations of oneself, or self-representations. The self-representations constitute the self-image, which becomes the main mental content that patterns our perception, our experience, of ourself. Our experience of ourselves becomes distorted by our representation of ourselves; we do not experience ourselves as as we truly are. In other words, because of the self-image our experience of ourselves is not objective; we experience ourselves through all the representations of ourselves, the representations that form the overall self-image.

We have said that spiritual realization is a matter of experiencing reality without representations. This experience is what we refer to then as Being; Being is contrasted to representing. So, in spiritual work we are basically working on seeing and penetrating representations to get to the reality underlying them. The point is to experience ourselves immediately, and not through the intermediacy of our representations of ourselves. Spiritual realization also means experiencing everything immediately, and not through the intermediacy of our representations. We experience everything then as Being, as thereness, as presence. More precisely, we use the term "Being" to refer to what is experienced when our awareness is not experiencing through the intermediacy of representations. Being is synonymous with true nature, which is the essence or ultimate nature.

A discovery that we may come upon in the process of seeing through representations is that the reality we experience through representations tends to be fixed and rigidly structured. This rigid structure blocks the openness that allows the dynamic flow, the true change and transformation of our experience of reality.

When we go through the representations things open up. We begin to see things more freely, in ways that are not determined by our previous experience, not determined by the representations in our minds. We become more open to experience, and our perception becomes lighter, clearer and more fluid. Things literally open up, meaning that when representations dissolve an open dimension of reality is revealed. This open dimension we call space. So it is not just that things become open in the psychological and metaphorical sense, but things are open in the sense that reality reveals a dimension of itself that is actually openness, that is actually spaciousness, that is literally space.

In other words, if our mind is experiencing things through representations our mind is closed and fixed. When the representations dissolve, there is literally openness, lightness and emptiness—space—in the mind.

We find out, as we penetrate our representations of reality, that space is a facet of Being. It is the openness of Being, or the open dimension of Being. We also discover that space is not only a manifestation of our being, of our true nature, but that it also deals directly with the question of representations. So space is the facet of our true nature that specifically and directly deals with the barrier of representations. The work on becoming aware of representations, seeing through and being free from them, has to do with the understanding of space.

The discussion in this book is primarily about self-image and its relation to space. Self-image is the representation of the self, but the realization of space is involved with the question of representation in general, not only the self-image. In dealing with any representation of anything, the question of space becomes important. More precisely, as we explore our experience from the perspective of how our representations determine that experience, Being manifests itself as space. Then we can experience the openness of our being as a boundless and infinite spaciousness, an empty and immaculate space coemergent with the awareness of it.

This experience of space then allows our being to manifest its essential qualities, the multicolored richness of its authentic and ontological presence. These are the spiritual qualities that are the source of our humanness, like love, compassion, peace, will, strength, truth, value and so on. In the course of this opening process, our experience becomes marked by the arising of these pure qualities, one of which is space.

This may lead us for a while to view space as one of the aspects, one of the qualities that emerge as we experience ourselves authentically. However, as our understanding matures, we realize that space is more fundamental—that space is an inherent facet of Being in general, that Being is always in reality characterized by openness. And when we are experiencing Being purely as this openness, we experience it as space, only space.

However, when we experience our being fully and completely, which can happen only in its deeper dimensions of manifestation, we realize there is no such thing as space that exists separately from other things. This separation is due to our underlying adherence to the mistaken view characteristic of the normal experience of physical space—that space and objects exist separately.

With this deeper understanding Being manifests space as its own openness, as its infinite spaciousness, that is inseparable from its presence. In other words, we realize that our experience of space is the experience of the spaciousness of the presence of Being. Ultimately, space cannot be separated from presence. More accurately, Being, which is presence, is inherently spacious and open. In other words, at every point of any manifestation, whether it is a physical object or an essential aspect, a thought or a feeling, there is space.

Space pervades all points, so that if we penetrate any point of any manifestation we will ultimately encounter space, the inner openness. Space is inherent in any manifestation of our Being, the way the back is inherent in the front. Space is the inside of any appearance, which is the outside. This is always true, as a fundamental truth of Being, but we can experience it directly only when our awareness is not obscured by representations.

One consequence of this is that, although each point is infinitesimal, its openness to space is infinite. In other words, each point is in contact with every other point, for the inside of each point is space, the very space that is the inside of all points. Pursuing this insight, we see that each point contains all other points. This indicates the nonlinearity of Being, where space is the inwardness of each point that opens it to the inwardness of every other point.

Another way of stating this subtle insight about our Being is that a point is not in space. We experience it ordinarily in a space, but the point itself is a manifestation of space. Space is an inherent quality of the point, and the moment we get in touch with this inherent quality we recognize that the point is really open, completely and totally open. In other words, space is the inherent openness of all reality. What representations do is to disconnect us from this inherent openness in any experience we have.

It is possible to see that space is present all the time, and that it underlies and inheres in any object that we perceive. So space becomes the inherent emptiness, the inherent openness in experience. That is why in some of the traditions, as that of Dzogchen, Being is described as having emptiness as its essence. Experientially, as we penetrate the representations through which we perceive, we discover that Being is presence whose essence is spaciousness. Our perception and understanding of spaciousness can go through degrees of refinement, which are experienced as the levels of space, until we recognize it with complete objectivity, which is possible when there are no obscurations in our experience of reality. At this subtlety of perception space and presence are so indistinguishable that experience becomes paradoxical. It is both being and nonbeing, both presence and absence, but not exactly, because even being and nonbeing are categories not free from representations. This is the dimension of the mystery of our Being.

Space is the inherent natural openness of experience, which has no bounds, no limitations. It is open through and through, in infinite ways and all dimensions. Being is not only open in three dimensions, it is open in all possible dimensions, to all possible experiences, which include the usual time and space. What we see as physical space is only the most obvious manifestation of this openness. This is the dimension of space which is the openness that allows physical objects to be.

This understanding leads us to the unity of Being, in which all manifestations are displays of Being, expressing and manifesting the same indivisible reality. Space is the openness of this nondual reality, acting to expose and dissolve the representations that usually occlude our awareness and prevent us from objectively perceiving it.

REFERENCES

Almaas, A.H., *Essence,* York Beach, Maine: Samuel Weiser, Inc., 1986.

Arasteh, Reza, *Growth to Selfhood,* London: Routledge & Kegan Paul, 1980.

Aurobindo, Sri, *On Himself,* Pondicherry, India: Sri Aurobindo Ashram Press, 1972.

Barrett, William, *Irrational Man,* New York: Doubleday & Company, Inc., 1962.

Blanck, Gertrude and Rubin, *Ego Psychology: Theory and Practice,* New York: Columbia University Press, 1974.

Blanck, Gertrude and Rubin, *Ego Psychology II,* New York: Columbia University Press, 1974.

Blum, Harold P., *Psychoanalytic Explorations of Technique,* New York: International Universities Press, Inc., 1980.

Edward, Joyce, et al., *Separation-Individuation,* New York: Gardner Press, Inc., 1981.

Evans-Wentz, W.Y., *The Tibetan Book of the Great Liberation,* New York: Oxford University Press, 1972.

Ferguson, John, *Encyclopaedia of Mysticism,* London: Thames and Hudson, 1976.

Freud, Sigmund, *The Ego and the Id,* New York: W.W. Norton & Company, Inc., 1962.

Freud, Sigmund, *The Problem of Anxiety,* New York: The Psycho-Analytic Quarterly Press and W.W. Norton & Company, Inc., 1963.

Guenther, Herbert V., *The Tantric View of Life,* Berkeley & London: Shambhala, 1972.

Guenther, Herbert V. and Trungpa, Chogyam, *The Dawn of Tantra,* Berkeley & London, 1975.

Guntrip, Harry, *Schizoid Phenomena, Object-Relations, and the Self,* New York: International Universities Press, Inc., 1969.

Hartmann, Heinz, *Ego Psychology and the Problem of Adaptation,* New York: International Universities Press, Inc., 1977.

Jacobson, Edith, *The Self and the Object World,* New York: International Universities Press, Inc., 1980.

Joshi, Vasant, *The Awakened One,* San Francisco: Harper and Row, Publishers, 1982.

Kernberg, Otto, *Borderline Conditions and Pathological Narcissism,* New York: Jason Aronson, 1975.

Kohut, Heinz, *The Analysis of the Self,* New York: International Universities Press, Inc., 1981.

Kohut, Heinz, *The Restoration of the Self,* New York: International Universities Press, Inc., 1981.

Krishnamurti, J., *Commentaries on Living, Second Series,* Wheaton, Illinois: The Theosophical Publishing House, 1981.

Mahler, Margaret S., et al., *The Psychological Birth of the Human Infant,* New York: Basic Books, Inc., Publishers, 1975.

Miller, Alice, *Prisoners of Childhood,* New York: Basic Books, Inc., Publishers, 1981.

Ouspensky, P. D., *In Search of the Miraculous,* New York: Harcourt, Brace and World, Inc., 1949.

Reich, Wilhelm, *Character Analysis,* New York: Simon and Schuster, 1971.

Reich, Wilhelm, *The Function of the Orgasm,* New York: Pocket Books of Simon and Schuster, 1978.

Trungpa, Chogyam, *Mudra,* Berkeley & London: Shambhala, 1972.

Trungpa, Chogyam, *Cutting Through Spiritual Materialism,* Boulder & London: Shambhala, 1973.

Tulku, Tarthang, *Time, Space, and Knowledge,* Emeryville, California: Dharma Publishing, 1977.

Winnicott, D.W., *The Maturational Processes and the Facilitating Environment,* New York: International Universities Press, Inc., 1980.

The Diamond Approach^{SM} is taught by Ridhwan teachers, certified by the Ridhwan Foundation. Ridhwan teachers are also ordained ministers of the Ridhwan Foundation. They are trained by DHAT Institute, the educational arm of the Ridhwan Foundation, through an extensive seven-year program, which is in addition to their work and participation as students of the Diamond Approach^{SM}. The certification process ensures that each person has a good working understanding of the Diamond Approach^{SM} and a sufficient capacity to teach it before being ordained and authorized to be a Ridhwan teacher.

The Diamond Approach^{SM} described in this book is taught in group and private settings in California and Colorado by Ridhwan teachers.

For information, write:

> Ridhwan
> P.O. Box 10114
> Berkeley, California 94709-5114

> Ridhwan School
> P.O. Box 18166
> Boulder, Colorado 80308–8166

Satellite groups operate in other national and international locations. For information about these groups, or to explore starting a group in your area, taught by certified Ridhwan teachers, write:

> Ridhwan
> P.O. Box 10114
> Berkeley, California 94709-5114